The Human Element
a guide to human behaviour in the shipping industry

MW01599413

Dedication

The global shipping industry is a dangerous place.
Every day, it loses two ships, pays out US$4 million in claims and radically
changes the lives of hundreds of people for ever.

Human behaviour is the source of virtually all such loss.
It is also the reason why the loss is not greater.

This book is dedicated to the professionalism of seafarers everywhere, and
to the growing number of seafaring organisations who want to know how
to guide human behaviour in a safer and more profitable direction.

Published by TSO (The Stationery Office) and available from:
**Online**
**www.tsoshop.co.uk**

**Mail, Telephone, Fax & E-mail**
TSO
PO Box 29, Norwich, NR3 1GN
Telephone orders/General enquiries: 0870 600 5522
Fax orders: 0870 600 5533
E-mail: customer.services@tso.co.uk
Textphone 0870 240 3701

**TSO@Blackwell and other Accredited Agents**

**Customers can also order publications from:**
TSO Ireland
16 Arthur Street, Belfast BT1 4GD
Tel 028 9023 8451 Fax 028 9023 5401

Published for the Maritime and Coastguard Agency under licence from the
Controller of Her Majesty's Stationery Office.



ISBN 978 0 11 553120 0

First published 2010



Printed in the United Kingdom for The Stationery Office
P002338036   C50   04/10

# Foreword

*We've heard many views on the 'human element' in the marine industry. The only thing that exceeds our use of the expression is our overall lack of understanding of it.*

*I sat an examination on human factors for my private pilot's licence. It was a revelation, saving me from potentially fatal consequences on at least one occasion.*

*I believe this book will go a long way to filling the knowledge gap in the shipping industry. It will not only help us run safer ships but more efficient ones as well. It should help convert the common belief that our officers and crews are our greatest hazard to the more accurate view that they are really our greatest asset.*

*I hope a well-thumbed copy will sit on the shelf of every ship and shipping office next to the 'Code of Safe Working Practice for Merchant Seamen'.*

*I am proud that we have been associated with this book's creation.*

**Martin Shaw**
*Vice President, Safety, Health, Marine & Engineering*
BP Shipping

*The safety of our seafarers and environment, and the way we learn, have been long-held passions of mine, so it is a source of great pride that Teekay Shipping has supported the MCA with this industry guide to human behaviour.*

*As an industry we need to start considering how decisions impact our seafarers. We need to consistently remember the past, both good and bad, and apply the lessons learned. This Guide helps us explore the way we learn, the way we work, the way we make decisions and the way we view risks.*

*In essence, it is a frame of reference for how to manage our people.*

*The Guide reveals the complex challenges associated with human behaviour. Insight into these will assist in maximising the skills of the many talented people in our industry.*

*People determine our industry's success – the first step starts with each one of us.*

**Captain Graham Westgarth**
*President*
Teekay Marine Services

*My experience as a Master at sea, and over 20 years ashore in ship management and ship operations, has made it clear to me that the major issue affecting the shipping industry today is the human element.*

*The technical issues have in the main been ironed out and the regulatory regime tightened up – but incidents and claims continue to occur.*

*The types of claim we see at the Standard Club keep recurring, and inevitably these are rooted in the more unfortunate consequences of human behaviour.*

*This book has the power to assist those people operating, managing and crewing the ships to address this major issue. I very much hope they seize the opportunities it provides.*

**Captain Chris Spencer**
*Director of Loss Prevention*
Standard P&I Club

*Shipping is a truly global industry through which international trade and much of the world economy flows. Some ships are the biggest self-propelled machines on the face of the earth. Yet ships and trade do not depend on vast machines – but on the people who run them.*

*More advances in the safety of seafarers and shipping are only possible through international cooperation, with national action on agreed standards. Securing maritime safety on behalf of the UK Government is our business at the Maritime and Coastguard Agency, the MCA. We know standards and inspections alone will not create a flourishing safety culture. We also need understanding of the source of safety – human behaviour.*

*This Guide offers an innovative and clear explanation of human behaviour across the maritime industry. It brings together a wealth of insight and good practice to help you run safer, more successful shipping.*

**Peter Cardy**
*Chief Executive*
Maritime and Coastguard Agency

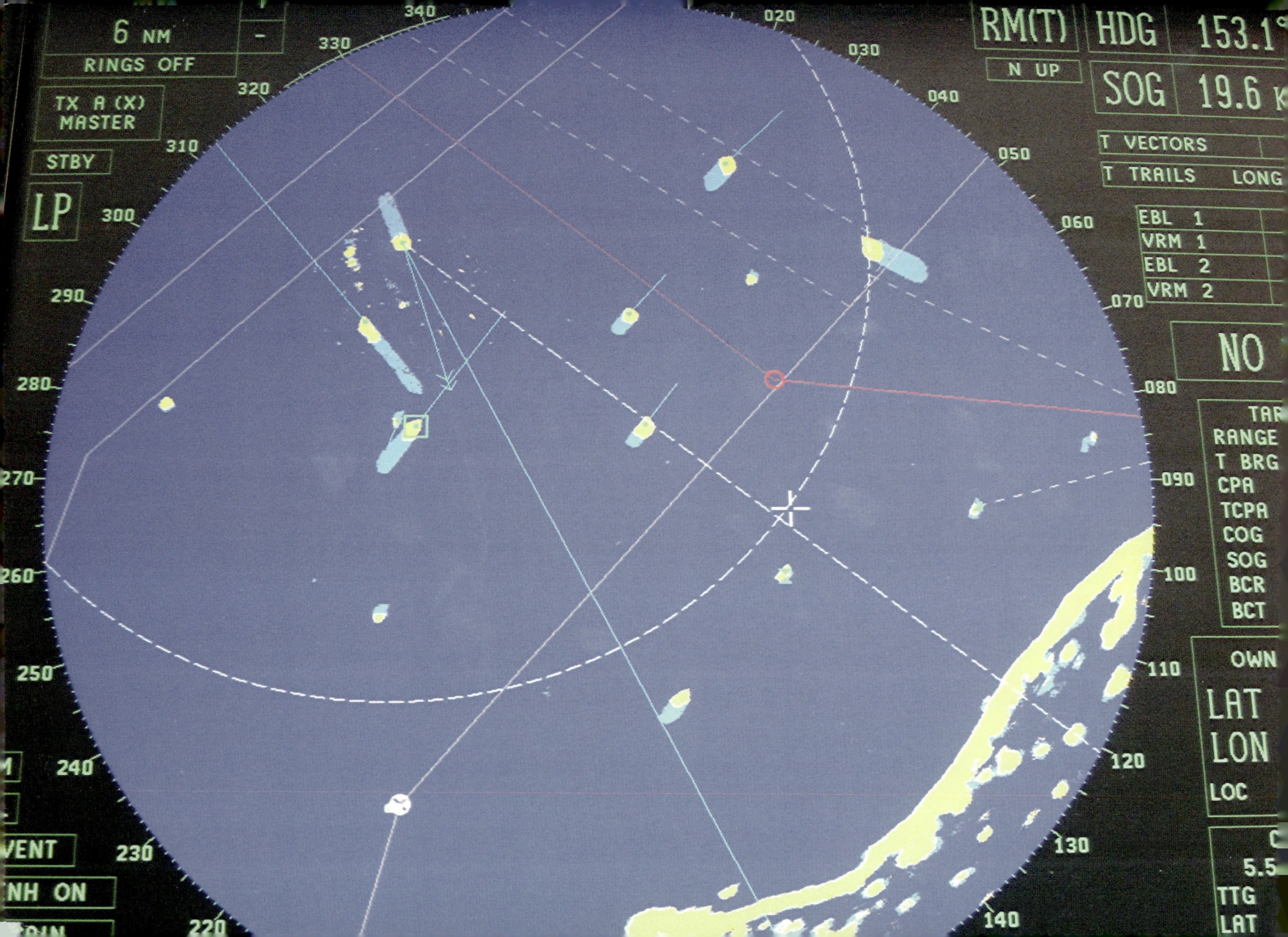
6 NM
RINGS OFF
TX A (X)
MASTER
STBY
LP
340
330
320
310
300
290
280
270
260
250
240
230
220
020
030
040
050
060
070
080
090
100
110
120
130
140
RM(T)
N UP
HDG
153.1°
SOG
19.6 K
T VECTORS
T TRAILS    LONG
EBL  1
VRM  1
EBL  2
VRM  2
NO
TAR
RANGE
T BRG
CPA
TCPA
COG
SOG
BCR
BCT
OWN
LAT
LON
LOC
5.5
TTG
LAT
VENT
NH ON

# About this Guide

### Who is this Guide for?

This Guide is aimed at:

- Masters and crews
- Owners and managers
- Designers and buyers
- Regulators and investigators

### What does it offer?

This Guide explains fundamental aspects of human behaviour, which together constitute what the commercial maritime sector calls 'the human element'. It makes clear that the human element is neither peripheral nor optional in the pursuit of a profitable and safe shipping industry. On the contrary, the capabilities and vulnerabilities of human beings are – and always will be – at the centre of the enterprise.

The Guide clearly shows that managing the human element must take place simultaneously at all levels of the industry – from within the engine rooms and decks of the smallest cargo ships to the conventions of the regulation makers and the boardrooms of the business strategists. It is the policies and strategies that shape and constrain the space in which ships and their crews operate.

The Guide offers insight, explanation and advice to help manage the human element more effectively.

### Why was it developed?

Analysis of shipping disasters in recent years has produced an increasing awareness of the central importance of the human element. The loss of life, the impact on company profits and credibility, and the vast environmental damage that can result from the loss of a vessel remain clear and present dangers.

Several recent initiatives have documented aspects of the human element, most notably ALERT!, a series of publications by Lloyds Register and the Nautical Institute. These are excellent resources that have been very successful in raising awareness about the importance of the human element. Because of these materials it is now widely understood that human issues are involved in almost all marine incidents. At the same time, the frequency of marine incidents continues unabated. It is not enough, it seems, to simply know that human issues are important.

It is now vital to make a clear connection between these human issues and the business success of those who make their living from the shipping industry – whether on ship or ashore. Specifically, everyone involved needs to understand that they, themselves, *are* the human element. Their continued business success depends on how far they are able to manage their own behaviour along with the behaviour of those around them.

This Guide was developed to help them do just that.

### How was it developed?

The Guide was designed and written by organisational psychologists Dik Gregory and Paul Shanahan. It is based on a wide range of consultations with maritime organisations, together with their own experience of creating related guidance materials for the defence, rail and air traffic control sectors.

The Guide was developed for the UK Maritime and Coastguard Agency and supported by BP Shipping, Teekay Marine Services and the Standard P&I Club.

# Contents

# Between the devil and the deep blue sea

### Sophie's choice

There was once a UK TV commercial for fried potato chips that featured two little sisters[1]. On the bus to school, the elder one mischievously asked the other: "Sophie, which do you prefer, Daddy or chips?" The question pre-occupied the little girl all day. "Daddy or chips? Daddy or chips?" she repeated to herself. She was still doing so when, back at home, she was served fish and chips for supper. Then, in came Daddy, who, with a peck on her cheek, stole a chip off her fork. She made her decision. "Chips," she announced with a rueful smile.

Fast forward a few years, and we find Sophie has now become the Finance Director for a shipping company operating in an increasingly competitive market. She has to advise on financial trade-offs between investment in automation and reduced manning, between the investment in staff and the shareholders' return on investment, between the costs of doing business and the savings that can be achieved across the company. Safety or profits? Safety or profits?

Fortunately for her company – and everyone in it – Sophie had long since realised that her sister's question had been a trick. She now knew that back then, chips were only on her plate at all because Daddy had been able to put them there. Daddy was the source of chips, not an alternative to them.

And so she broke free from the choice between the devil and the deep blue sea[2]. She knew that profits flowed from safety, and that without safety, profits would be hard to come by. But how was she able to convince her Board and the company shareholders of this insight?

### Putting it all above board

First she collected some key facts[3]:

- In 1997, a P&I Club reported that human error dominated the underlying causes of major claims. It was responsible for 58% of all such claims – a figure that has not changed for ten years. Over the same period, the other main cause – ship failure – had decreased by two-thirds.

- In the five years to 2005, an average of 18 ships collided, grounded, sank, caught fire or exploded *every single day*. Incredibly, two ships sank every day.

- The Standard P&I Club estimates that over a recent ten-year period, insurance claims cost the P&I industry US$15 billion. *That's US$4 million dollars every single day.* Over 65% of this vast payout – an amazing US$10 billion – was for incidents in which humans played the dominant part.

- The International Union of Marine Insurance (IUMI) declared 2006 to be a catastrophic year for hull claims. The next year, it was four times worse.

- IUMI reports the average number of incidents involving the serious or total loss of vessels over 500gt had steadily risen in the 15-year period to 2008. 60% of these – around two major incidents per day in 2008 – were due to human error.

- In 2008, a maritime disaster occurred nearly every week (on average). Each one involved an insurance claim of over US$17m or had an economic impact of over US$85m.

- In 2008, maritime insurers paid out over half a billion US dollars for casualties.

- The cost of acquiring a new ship is anything from US$50m for a general cargo ship to US$250m for a fully equipped LNG tanker. In 2009, the renewal costs for the International Group of P&I Clubs increased by an average of 16.5%.

- P&I Clubs are conducting much more wide-ranging member risk reviews as a condition of insurance and premium calculation. These reviews now examine the quality and effectiveness of management and leadership ashore, shipboard personnel, change, accident and near-miss analysis and loss prevention.

- Ship operating costs vary from US$2 to 20 million per year. If a ship is damaged in an accident, these costs can no longer be offset by its trading revenue. When the cruise ship *Royal Majesty* grounded in 1995, it cost US$5 million in just 14 days lost revenues. Furthermore, operating costs are radically increased by the cost of unplanned repairs, legal bills, third-party compensation, environmental cleanup, knock-on effects such as refinery shut-down due to a delayed tanker, and loss of commercial reputation. The final costs for the 1989 *Exxon Valdez* disaster were US$4 billion.

---

[1] McCain Foods Ltd (1998), re-told here with permission

[2] In sailing warships, the devil was the seam that sealed the main deck to the hull. Anyone repairing this crucial seam was required to hang dangerously over the side of the ship, literally between the devil and the deep blue sea.
[3] From IUMI, Lloyds Register, BP Shipping, Teekay Marine Services, Standard P&I Club.

- Studies from the software and air traffic control industries[4] show that investing in the right design saves up to 100 times the costs compared to fixing problems later – a most noteworthy fact for shipowners and designers alike.

## Knowing which way the wind blows

Sophie created a diagram so that she could see how things actually influenced her company's fortunes. You can see part of Sophie's diagram opposite.

It showed her how all of the elements were connected as a single, though complex, system. Changing any one of them could, potentially, affect all the others. Sometimes there would be a system lag – much as a helmsman's heading alteration takes time to change the ship's course. But the effect would always occur at some stage – sometimes with profound consequences.

The diagram shed new light on the workings of the 'law of unintended consequences'. She couldn't use it to predict exactly what would happen – or when – but somehow she felt she had given herself a better view of the seas through which her company was navigating. In particular, she was able to see that everything had an upside as well as a downside, and that some of the relationships were vicious circles. For example:

- Investment in training could decrease risk taking, workload, fatigue and stress, which could in turn reduce the number of adverse incidents. But without an effective competency verification scheme, it could also encourage faster Officer promotion, resulting in decreased crew competence through insufficient experience, and thereby, *more* adverse incidents and lost profits.

- Investment in automation could produce leaner, more efficient operations. But without an increase in training investment, it could also increase risk taking, require better recruits, and lead to less safe manning levels through the apparent need for fewer crew – all leading to increased adverse incidents and further company expense.

- Increased rules, regulations, standards and codes arising from the response to adverse incidents would emphasise the role of regulatory authorities and increase the pressure on shipowners to improve the measurable quality of their operations. But this, in turn, could increase the need for compliance, increase company costs, and increase risk-taking (through the search for compensating efficiencies), workload, fatigue and stress, which in turn could increase the numbers of adverse incidents and loss of profits.

- Investment in better working, social and living conditions could be achieved by designing better ships and safer (higher) manning levels. It could also help attract higher calibre recruits, increase seafarer quality and decrease the company's exposure to problems of risk taking, workload, fatigue and stress and, thereby, costly adverse incidents. However, financial pressures on the company to become leaner and more efficient could once again worsen seafarers' living and working conditions and increase the risk taking, workload, fatigue and stress of the crew, leading to more adverse incidents and loss of profits.

Sophie was able to show the Board that the behaviour of staff, Masters and crews usually flowed along the course of least resistance. In turn, this course was determined by their human capacities; their expertise; the expectations, management style and culture of the company; and the requirements of the law.

If behaviour was unsafe, it was because the company – and the system it was part of – was wrongly configured.

She pointed out that management could influence the system that produced the behaviour in their company in several important ways, eg:

- *Working within the capacities and limitations of its staff.* The company could accommodate these in its policies and operational practices – but only if it could understand them sufficiently well in the first place.

- *Optimising the amount of expertise available to it.* The company could do this through its monitoring of staff performance, learning and development; through its investment in mentoring and training; and through its reputation as an employer of quality to attract and retain sufficient numbers of new and higher calibre staff.

- *Effectively transmitting a realistic set of expectations.* The company's expectations needed to be based on a practical understanding of the human realities of seafaring, as well as giving staff the confidence that they would be fairly supported when things went wrong, eg by means of a 'just culture'.

---

[4] For example, Eurocontrol (1999)

- *Assuring the requirements of the law and associated regulations*. The company needed to develop evidence-based knowledge of actual operational practices; to seek active representation on professional committees, maritime conventions and the International Maritime Organisation (IMO); and to lobby Insurance Clubs, Classification Societies and Government in order to seek changes in policy that better reflected the human requirements of its workforce.

Sophie's fellow Board members found themselves fully engaged with their need to understand how to actively nourish the roots of their own profitability – ie the behaviour, motivations, capabilities and strengths of the people they employed.

So Sophie invited her Board to pay serious attention to the contents of this Guide, where she felt sure they would find the insight and new perspective they needed.

## Sophie's world

In drawing her diagram, Sophie connected topics with red arrows if she saw that a topic reduced what it pointed at. And she used blue arrows if a topic increased what it pointed at.

As she followed the arrows around, she spotted a number of circular relationships that captured both advantages and disadvantages. Some of these are described opposite.

If you follow some of the arrows, you may spot other circularities. They show how decisions in one area will have unintended consequences in other areas unless the whole picture is considered as a single system.

### Sophie's world of circular causality

This 'circular causality' reflects some of the relationships that decision makers must work with in the real world of company trade-offs. For reasons of space, not all topics and links are shown.

### How to read blue arrows

The *more* of the source topic, then the *more* of the destination topic.

### How to read red arrows

The *more* of the source topic, then the *less* of the destination topic. Or, if you prefer, the *less* of the source topic, then the *more* of the destination topic.

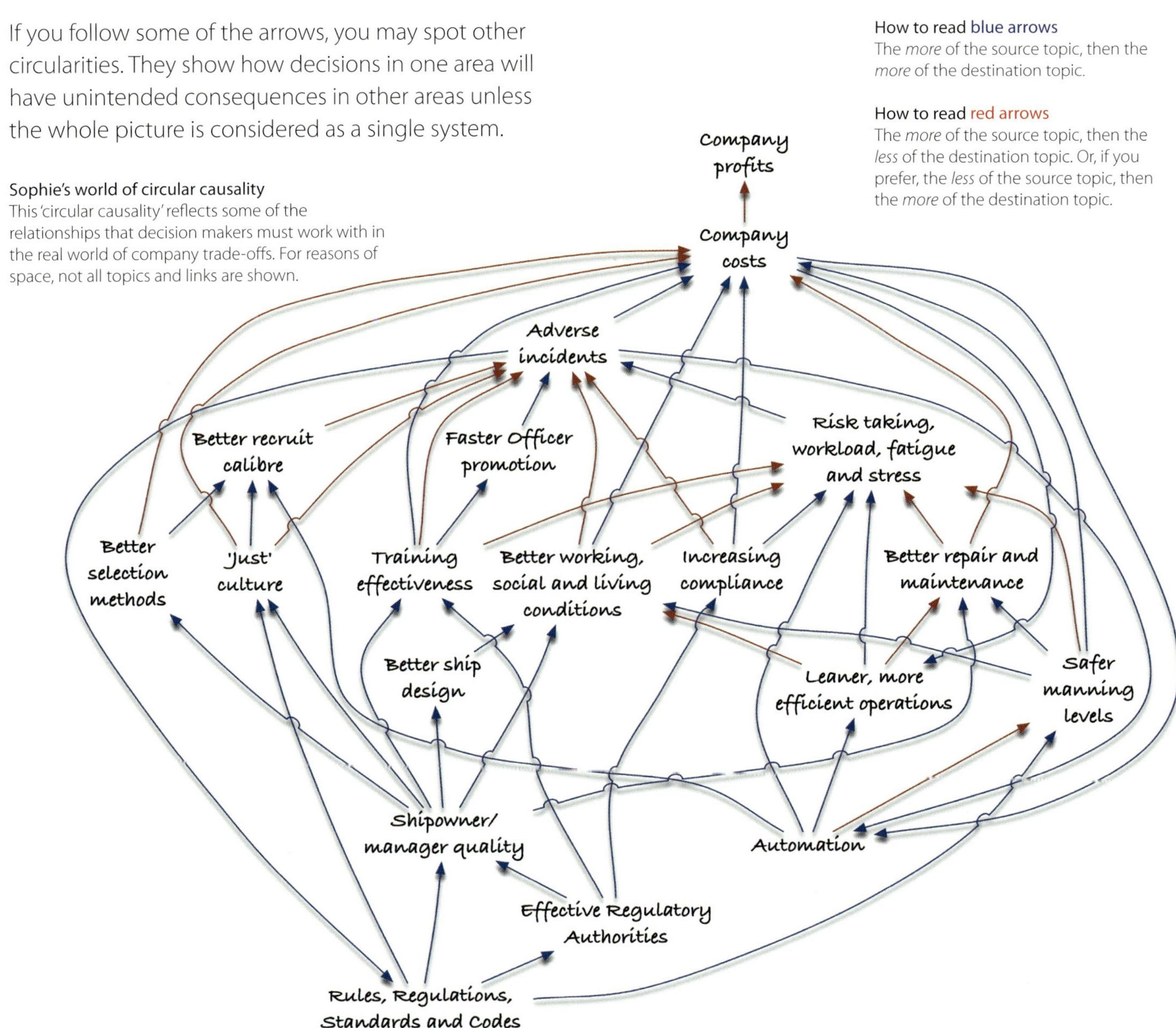

# Getting under way

## What is the human element?

The shipping industry is run by people, for people. People design ships, build them, own them, crew them, maintain them, repair them and salvage them. People regulate them, survey them, underwrite them and investigate them when things go wrong.

While these people vary in all sorts of ways, they are all, nevertheless, people – with the same basic set of capabilities and vulnerabilities.

The 'human element' is misnamed. It implies something that happens at the sidelines – a piece of the picture that is hopefully being dealt with by some specialist or other. Or else it implies that it's 'just one of those things' – a bit of a mystery about which we can do little more than shrug our shoulders and hope for the best.

But humans are not simply an element like the weather. They are at the very centre of the shipping enterprise. They are the secret of its successes and the victims of its failures. It is human nature that drives what happens every day at work – from the routine tasks of a ship's rating, right through to the policy decisions of the IMO.

Fortunately, there is a lot that is known about human nature – and a lot of practical things that can be done to ensure people play to their strengths – while avoiding the pitfalls. So, what do we mean by human nature? The compass rose on this page points to eight basic aspects of human nature that we explore in this Guide.

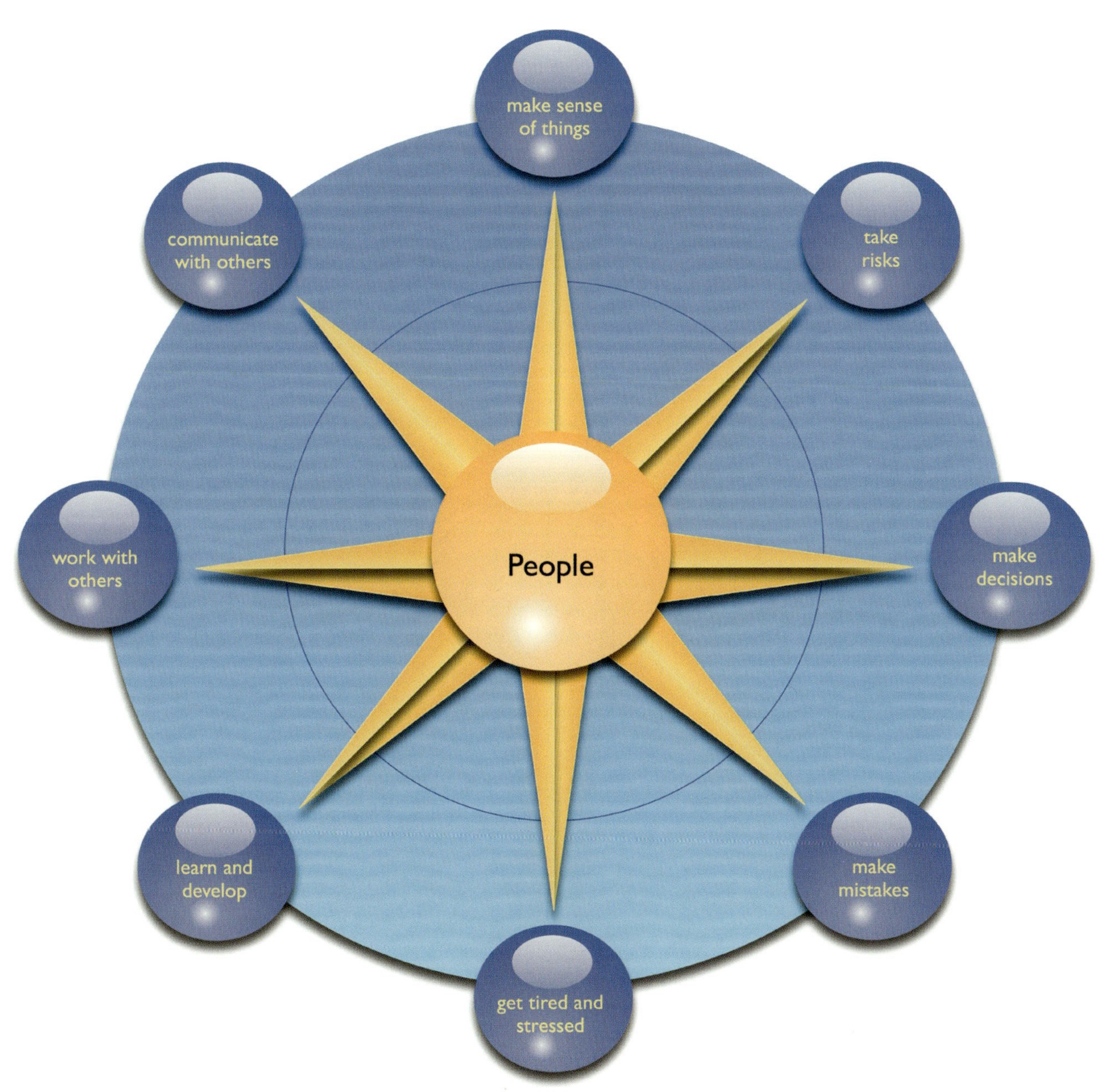

## Charting the course

This Guide shows you how to navigate through the deep waters indicated by each compass point. It illustrates what each one really means, together with common myths, misunderstandings, Dos and Don'ts. Most importantly, it shows you how you can set a better course through each one – and what is risked when not enough attention is paid to them *en route*.

There are many insights that this Guide can give you. Having these insights means that you will navigate the human element more knowledgeably, more safely and more enjoyably. And because of that, you will help your organisation to achieve its business goals more efficiently and more profitably.

You can make an immediate human element appraisal of your own company or ship by e-mailing the MCA Human Element Team at *human.element@mcga.gov.uk* and asking them about their Human Element Assessment Tool (HEAT).

The eight aspects of human nature examined in this Guide are introduced on these two pages.

## 1 People actively make sense of things

What's obvious to you may be far from apparent to somebody else. We explain how it is that most of what you see and understand is down to you and your expectations, rather than a response to 'what's out there'. The key problem is ensuring that the sense you make of things is enough for you to deal effectively with the reality of a continuously unfolding situation – a situation that you must also share with your colleagues.

## 2 People take risks

Everybody takes risks all the time. In a world that is essentially uncertain, this is not only normal but inescapable. We explain how the human perception of risk is quite different from the probability with which events actually occur. The key problem is in ensuring that your own perception of risk maps well onto the world with which you are interacting.

## 3 People make decisions

We explain the difference between how people think they make decisions and how they actually do it – and how experts' decision making is quite different from the way they did it when they were learning. We also explain why experience does not always lead to expertise, but that expertise always requires experience – and lots of it. The key problem is to understand what the components of a good decision are, and how to recognise when you are about to make a bad one.

## 4 People make mistakes

A fundamental human strength depends directly on the ability to make, and then recover from, mistakes. Without error there can be no learning or development. And without these, organisations cannot achieve their goals. The main problem here is in ensuring that potentially harmful or expensive mistakes are prevented, caught or minimised before they have a chance to get far enough to matter. We explain how this depends as much on organisational culture as on individual competence.

## 5 People get tired and stressed

We explain the causes and consequences of fatigue and stress, and explain what you can do to avoid them or lessen their impact. We also explain why workload turns out to be as much to do with your own experience, as the actual demands placed on you by the job.

## 6 People learn and develop

People learn all the time. They can't stop themselves. The main problem is in ensuring that you learn the right things at the right time. People also have aspirations which can be managed by an organisation to further its own safety and profitability. However, in the absence of good management, people's aspirations will either be ignored or permitted to dominate – with potentially disastrous consequences either way. We explain the enormous power that effective, well-timed training can give to an organisation.

### 7 People work with each other

Working with each other sometimes requires us to work as individuals in pursuit of our own goals, and at other times as members of a team with a common purpose. Either way, the key problem is in ensuring that we have effective 'people' skills – as well as technical task skills. We explain what these other skills are, why they are important and what can go wrong when they are absent.

### 8 People communicate with each other

Successful communication involves the clear transmission of a message, right? Actually this is only a part of the story. We explain what has to happen for communication to be successful. We explain the responsibilities of both listener and messenger – and how apparently successful communication can continue for long periods until disaster suddenly strikes, all because both parties were inhabiting completely different worlds of their own construction.

### Battening down

These are eight things we do that help to make us human. They are inescapable and will not go away. Understanding a little more about their nature, and how you can deal with them more effectively, will change your behaviour – and, maybe, that of those around you.

And this is just what we hope, because everything you do – together with the behaviour of all your colleagues both ashore and afloat – *is* the human element.

It can either work for you or against you!



### Weighing anchor

The contents of this Guide are based on the findings of a great many researchers of human behaviour. While we won't overburden you with our many sources, the key work of our professional colleagues is referenced along the way and in the *Bibliography*. Please take a look there if you would like further information about any of the topics we explore.

This Guide is meant for browsing, and you are invited to read its sections in any order. However, we suggest you start by heading north with the first section, since it is a main reference point for the other seven headings.

Whatever order you choose, we hope that the information is of immediate value to you and that the advice we provide will assist you to your next port of call even more safely and enjoyably than your last.

So let's weigh anchor, choose a compass heading and make for the open sea!

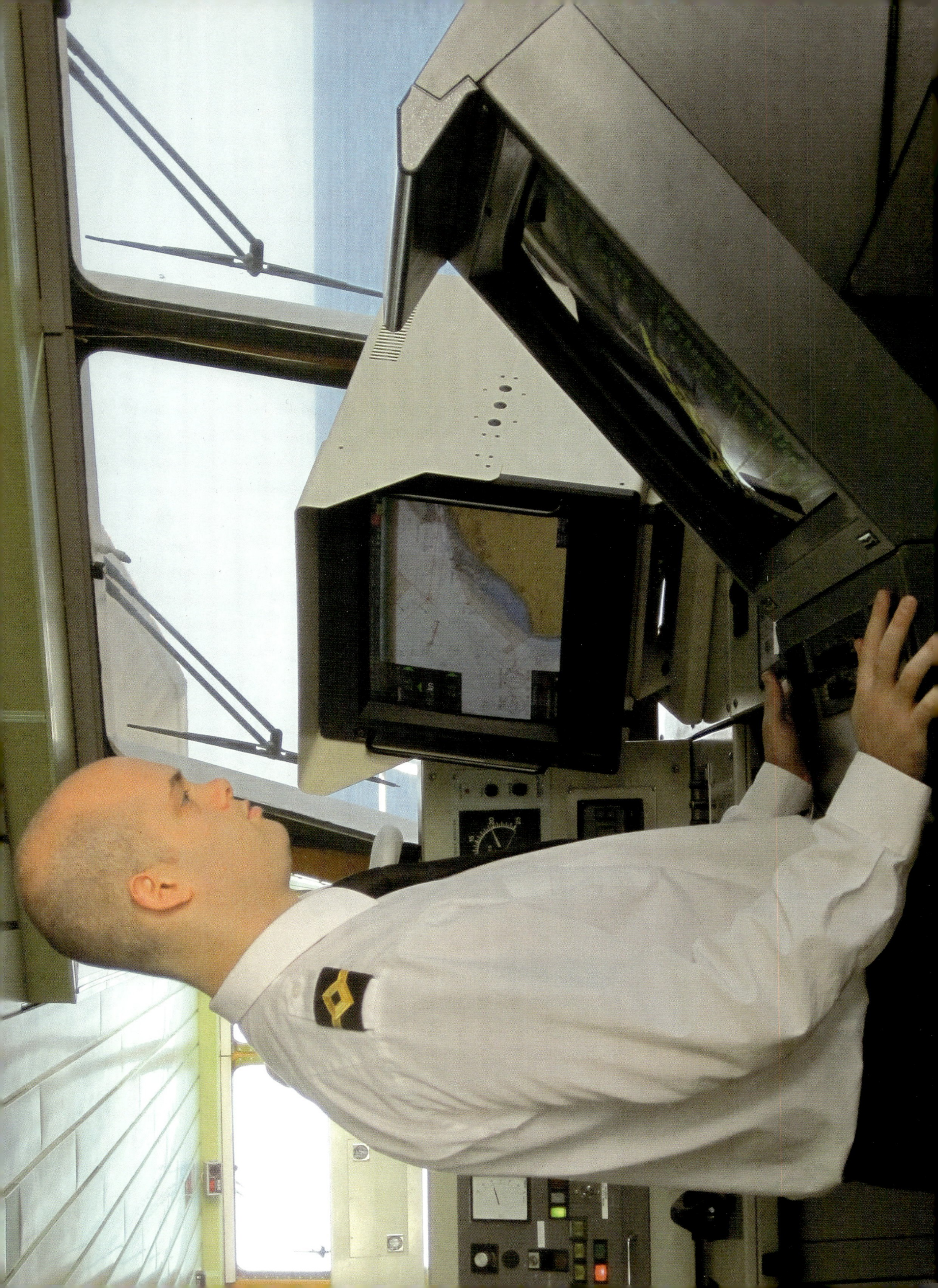

# Making sense of things

## What's the situation?

Uncertainty, ambiguity and complexity are normal characteristics of our world. This world is also filled with vast amounts of information. While our five senses connect us with the world, the selection of the information we pay attention to, and the sense we make of it, happens largely in our heads (see panel, *Sensing and making sense: what's the difference?*).

We strive to make sense of things in order to make the world sufficiently certain to support our goals, plans and activities. We also use sense-making to modify our plans when the world breaks through anyway – because these plans can never completely deal with its uncertainty, ambiguity and complexity.

Human beings impose sense on the world. Most of the time, they see what they expect to see. Furthermore, since each person's sense-making is a unique property of their physiology, self concept and culture, experience, and social and intellectual needs, each person essentially inhabits a situation that is different from everyone else's.

Our ability to share situations, goals and meaning depends on two other key human properties: empathy and communication. Empathy is a particular and powerful form of human imagination. People refer to it as 'putting themselves in another's shoes'. It is what

> ## "We have met the enemy, and he is us."
>
> Pogo, from the pen of Walt Kelly, 1953

makes teamworking (see section on *Working with others*) possible and is concerned with glimpsing enough of another's perspective to understand how to support the achievement of mutual goals. Communication (see section *Communicating with others*) is the mechanism by which we express empathy.

Let's look at what happened when three different crews all made different sense of the same information.

## Case study: A collision between three situations[1]

In early March 1999, *Hoo Robin*, a hardworking coaster, left her berth in the River Trent to sail down river, bound for Antwerp on a ballast voyage. On the bridge were her Master and Mate, while the three remaining crew, two ABs and an AB/Cook, settled down to a meal. The visibility was good, it was just getting dark and it was nearing the end of the flood tide. Ahead of *Hoo Robin*, sailing up the river in the opposite direction, were four other vessels. Two would be passed without incident. The third was *Arklow Marsh* with a cargo of 2,015 tonnes of bulk phosphates. Half a mile behind the *Arklow Marsh* was *Ara*.

As he steered down the river, *Hoo Robin's* Master was aware that just a month before he had been involved in a passing that had gone wrong. On that occasion he had been coming the other way, inbound, when he radioed an outbound vessel to request a red to red passing so that the ships would pass

[1] Based on MAIB (1999) with further interpretation by the authors

<table>
<tr><td>

**Sensing and making sense: what's the difference?**

It is easy to assume that the five human senses simply capture the world and, somehow, store it in memory for later use – much like a video. If it was really like this, we would of course quickly drown in a vast sea of data. Just like a Master on a ship with a passage to make, we need the means to get our bearings, and navigate a course that has some meaning and value for us.

While it is the five senses through which information is collected, it is the context we create for ourselves that mainly controls what we pay attention to and create meaning for.

Our memory of an event is also highly dependent on the context in which we sensed and interpreted it. Human memory is not like a hard drive or video tape that simply stores information. It is a medium used to structure and retain the *meaning* that events have for us. And unlike video tape, human memory does not simply play back what was put there. It is always influenced by the new context we are in when we try to remember.

Our pre-occupation with what is important at the time, and what things mean – both then, and later – helps explain why two people can have very different experiences of the same event. It also helps explain why they give different accounts of it later. The fact is that no two people are ever in the same situation as each other. And neither are they in the situation experienced by a third party, such as an accident investigator, who is trying to understand their behaviour at a later time.

Human senses are physiological marvels, but they are not of central importance in this Guide. Instead, our focus here is on how we create context and meaning for ourselves – in short, not how we sense, but how we make sense.

</td></tr>
</table>

each other on their port sides. The other ship had replied requesting instead a green to green passing – not uncommon on that stretch of the river. *Hoo Robin's* Master had agreed, but in altering course to make way for the other vessel, he had run aground.

Now, with the Mate on the bridge with him, *Hoo Robin's* Master negotiated with, and then passed the first two of the inbound ships red to red. Aware that the Mate needed some food and rest before taking the next watch, the Master sent him below.

Alone on the bridge he could see the two remaining inbound ships ahead of him, *Arklow Marsh*, followed by *Ara*. As was customary, all ships were broadcasting their positions as they passed key points on the river. The crew on *Arklow Marsh* could see *Hoo Robin* ahead showing a green sidelight. They naturally assumed there would be a green to green passing. At that moment, *Hoo Robin's* Master assessed the nearer *Arklow Marsh* to be at the point known as Hillside, with *Ara* at the point known as Cliff End. In order to make contact with the nearer of the two, he called "the vessel approaching Hillside". *Arklow Marsh* was the nearer vessel, but was already well past Hillside, so she didn't respond. *Ara* was approaching Hillside, though still half a mile from it. *Ara* responded to *Hoo Robin* and agreed a red to red passing.

So, *Hoo Robin's* Master had now agreed a red to red passing with the furthest ship, believing it to be the nearest ship. None of the three ships' crews had any clue that they had completely different understandings of the same set of events. *Hoo Robin* altered her course sharply to starboard to accommodate the red to red passing with the nearest ship. But the nearest ship continued under the assumption of a

green to green. As the three parties began to glimpse *Hoo Robin's* confusion between *Arklow Marsh* and *Ara*, *Ara's* Pilot – through radio interference – began to explain the situation as he saw it. Against the crackling of the radio, *Hoo Robin's* Master heard the word 'green' and altered course hard to port for a green to green passing. At the same time, *Arklow Marsh* went hard to starboard to effect the red to red originally intended by *Hoo Robin*. Seconds later, *Arklow Marsh's* bow ploughed into *Hoo Robin's* starboard side, causing costly damage and delay to both vessels. Fortunately, there were no injuries or pollution.

As is usual, several factors were found to have played their part in this accident, including fatigue, excess workload and ineffective radio procedure. But there were also some key sense-making factors, too. These were that:

- What *Hoo Robin's* Master thought he saw with his own eyes provided such compelling evidence that radio broadcasts about the other vessels' actual location were ignored. It was obvious to him which ship he was talking to – but then only he was in his own situation. Of course, the same was true for each of the others.

- Each of the three participants selected bits of information to make sense of the situation as they saw it. It is a lot easier for humans to seek confirming evidence for their current understanding than to test it and risk having to invest significant effort in devising another explanation.

- Even at the last moment, when things suddenly became less certain, the Master of *Hoo Robin* seized upon fragmentary evidence (the word 'green') to decide on the most plausible course of action. This plausibility came from the green aspect of *Arklow Marsh* combined with *Hoo Robin's* grounding the month before: her Master's recent experience provided a sensible context for aiming for deeper water – but then no-one else shared that context.

## How do we make sense of things?

So how do we make sense of what our senses tell us? There are a number of factors that determine what we pay attention to, and how we use this information to interpret the world around us.

These include:

- Our personal needs

- Our self-concept

- Our past experience

- The goals we share with others

- Our current practicalities

Let's look at each of these in turn.

No-one had a clue they had completely different understandings of the same event...

## Our personal needs

In order to deal with the constant bombardment on our senses, we need some way of filtering the huge amount of available information. As we mature, it seems we develop a hierarchy of mental filters[2] based on our needs. The most basic filters are concerned with our own survival. We get hungry, thirsty and tired. These demand attention on a frequent and regular basis, forcing solutions to be found. If we try to ignore these basic needs, they quickly come to completely dominate behaviour.

When *Hoo Robin's* Master sent his ABs and then his Mate below to eat, he was paying attention to their personal needs in the light of the forthcoming demands of the sea voyage. Meanwhile, although he was tired himself, the practicalities of his schedule dictated that he stayed on the bridge to carry out the river navigation to the sea.

A sudden, shocking event – like a loud noise or alarm – will usually interrupt whatever we are doing so that we may decide whether to confront the threat or escape from it. This 'fight or flight' reaction automatically (and rather sensibly) grabs our full attention in an attempt to preserve our safety. It is triggered in a very old part of the brain that is also responsible for emotions, such as anger, fear and happiness.

The advantage is that this part of our brain works very fast – even before we are consciously aware of what we are responding to. The problem is that we don't have direct access to the emotional life it produces. These emotions are always present as a background to conscious life, colouring it and helping to provide the foundation for what we attend to and the way we interpret what we see. A good example of this is the so-called 'halo effect'. This means that if you view someone favourably on some aspect such as trustworthiness, you usually view them positively on other aspects – eg kindness, honesty and professional competence – even when there is no direct evidence for these. There is also something called the 'horns effect' which works the opposite way, resulting in generally negative perceptions of other people.

As we develop, we use more sophisticated attentional filters. One filter relates to our need for acceptance by social groups that we value, eg family, friends and colleagues. Another type of filter is concerned with recognition by our peers for our personal achievements. The most advanced filter is one concerned with examining the world for what it can contribute to our own growth and development – for the purposes of personal fulfilment.

Each of the filters brings into focus a different set of goals that compete for our attention. To make things more complicated, the filters interact with each other. For example, as a seafarer you can – up to a point – choose to ignore your fatigue or hunger on a task in deference to a need for acceptance by your fellow crew members, or recognition by management. Serious problems can arise in organisations which, inadvertently or otherwise, permit higher level filters to take precedence over lower ones.

> **People filter out most of the information around them.**

Other sections in this Guide (*Getting tired and stressed* and *Taking risks*) contain several examples of this. In the case of *Hoo Robin's* Master, it is possible to glimpse several of these filters in operation – including basic needs (ie personal fatigue); social acceptance (ie managing the basic needs of the crew); and peer recognition (ie progressing the ship on the sea voyage planned by its owners).

## Our self-concept

Each of us has a sense of who we are and what we are like. This sense of personal identity is developed through contact with family, friends, workmates, supervisors, management and, ultimately, by the working and ethnic cultures in which we live. Cultural differences are particularly relevant in the maritime world due to the involvement of several major seafaring nations. We'll look at aspects of these differences in several other sections of this Guide, as well as here in the panel, *How does a person's culture affect their sense-making?*

---

[2] Maslow (1943)

Your private views on where you fit and what you are capable of have a powerful impact on the sense you make of the situations in which you find yourself. For example, your sense of self may influence how much you feel you can initiate communication with another, or listen to what you are being told. It helps determine the extent to which you submit to authority or expect to negotiate with it. It shapes your approach to teamworking, and it influences the kind of leader you are, both of which in turn influence the sense you make of the events you share with others.

Other sections in this Guide (*Communicating with others* and *Working with others*) give examples. In the case of *Hoo Robin*, it is likely that her Master's experience in her grounding a month before produced some self-doubt about negotiating passings. The accident investigators certainly regarded it as noteworthy that he unnecessarily overloaded both himself and the VHF channel by contacting every approaching vessel to ask if they wanted a non-standard passing.

## Our past experience

The conclusions and reflections that we generate from our past experience play a big part in shaping the sense we make of the present. This past experience may consist of beliefs, mental models, rules, procedures and stories that we apply to features of the present environment to render it meaningful. The more experience we have, the more likely we are to recognise the present as familiar. But note that any familiarity we notice is a projection we have made from our own past. By the same token, there is no good reason why anyone else is able to make the same projection and so attach the same meaning to a situation.

Sometimes, the failure to appreciate this in the seafaring world results in particular types of incident – especially collisions such as *Hoo Robin* and *Arklow Marsh*. In this case, the past grounding experience of *Hoo Robin's* Master filtered his attention in a number of ways:

- First, it made him focus too intently on getting each passing right – to the point where he got it wrong by overlooking more relevant information such as the actual locations the other ships were broadcasting.

- Second, the emergency change to a green passing that had taken place a month before may have influenced him to regard the word 'green' that he heard on this occasion as significant.

- Third, his past grounding experience helped provide his 'gut-feeling' decision, taken in the last minute, to aim for deeper water – straight into the path of *Arklow Marsh*.

> Expertise requires experience, but does not automatically follow from it.

Further problems can arise if we confuse experience with expertise. They are not the same thing at all. For example, a person's experience may result in wrong conclusions and bad practice; or it may not yet be sufficient, leading to over-confidence, inadvertent risk taking and complacency. Another section of this Guide deals with the problem of risk and what factors affect our perception of it (see section on *Taking risks*).

The importance of the role of experience in the decisions we make is addressed in another section (*Making decisions*). In this we will look at the differences between experience and expertise and how expert decision making in operational settings is not the considered, option-weighing process that many believe it to be.

## Our shared goals

We are helped to make sense of a situation if we are engaged with each other in pursuing a common goal. What seems to be important is that we agree joint goals, refine our understanding, take action and maintain a balance to our activities within a shared operation such as crewing a ship or managing a shipping company. It is the shared goal-based context of these activities that provides big clues about how to make sense of what's happening at any moment.

Goal-sharing can be helped considerably by training aimed at helping people to develop shared methods, together with a realistic understanding of each other's roles and capabilities. Problems arise when the goals of people in the same organisation begin to diverge. A good example of this is when safety considerations appear to conflict with profit-making. This can happen, for example, when shareholders' shorter-term views are allowed undue significance.

> Problems arise when the goals of people in the same organisation start to diverge.

In the case of *Hoo Robin*, everyone obviously had the shared goal of avoiding a collision. However, on the day, this goal failed to be grounded in a proper agreement or shared method. Instead, the overall goal gave way to different goals demanding different methods. The Master of *Hoo Robin* was (over-)using the VHF radio to try to achieve his goal of preventing ambiguity (ironically causing the very thing he was trying to prevent). Meanwhile, untroubled by previous incidents, the crew of *Arklow Marsh* were using visual sightings to assume a green to green passing with *Hoo Robin*. For them, as for the crew of *Ara*, the potential for ambiguity was not a dominant consideration.

When one perspective is permitted to dominate others, it not only indicates that goals cease to be shared, but that sub-goals (eg safety or profit; seeking to avert ambiguity or seeking a straightforward passing) are being mistaken for overall goals. If this situation is allowed to continue, failure occurs. The same is true for different organisations which are part of the same enterprise, such as the shipping industry as a whole. For example, if the regulators end up dominating the operations of the shipowners (or *vice-versa*), then the whole enterprise will become dysfunctional. Another section of this Guide deals with leadership, teamworking and shared goals (*Working with others*), while other sections (*Taking risks* and *Making mistakes*) deal with the consequences of organisational problems in this area.

## Our need to be practical

In any situation where we have things to achieve, we do not have infinite amounts of time and usually have a strong sense of diminishing returns (see section on *Making decisions*). In making sense of things, we usually stop when we have enough information to decide on a course of action that seems plausible. Our preference is for a working level of understanding rather than a search for absolute truth. For example, when faced with uncertainty or too much information, an Officer of the Watch (OOW) will simplify their information needs to support a decision that seems workable in the time available. This may or may not turn out to be sufficient to deal with the reality of the unfolding event.

There are many maritime examples where available information from modern bridge technology turns out to be ignored. Training can help, but it needs to be highly effective to overcome people's overwhelming need for simplicity in times of crisis.

In the case of *Hoo Robin's* Master, he seized on something meaningful to him – the word 'green' – from the complicated and difficult-to-hear explanation from *Ara* over the radio, and used it to decide the most plausible action – for him – in the time available. We will return to this aspect again in the sections on *Making decisions*, *Getting tired and stressed* and *Making mistakes*.

## How much of a problem is sense-making?

Inappropriate sense-making is a large and costly problem for the shipping industry – whether measured in lost profits, fines, investigation, legal and insurance costs, environmental damage, or sheer human misery.

### Case study: Fatal collision on Chesapeake Bay[3]

In 1978 the US Coastguard training cutter *Cuyahoga* was travelling at full speed north in Chesapeake Bay. Travelling at full speed towards them was *Santa Cruz II*, a large cargo ship. *Cuyahoga's* Captain saw two lights, indicating the ship ahead was travelling in the same direction. He explained to himself that the fast closing speed on his radar was because he was overtaking a fishing vessel. Meanwhile his other crew had seen three lights and knew the vessel was approaching them.

No communication was attempted between these crew members and their Captain since there was no clue that they had interpreted things differently.



Just before impact, their Captain blew his whistle, apparently confirming their belief he was aware of the same situation as them. He was not. He blew the whistle to accompany a hard turn to port to give the other vessel more space as – so he thought – both ships approached the Potomac river. *Cuyahoga* was impaled by a ship four times its length on her starboard side and 11 coastguardsmen lost their lives.

Sense-making is a significant factor in virtually all marine incidents, which remain numerous. Lloyds Register tells us that between 1995 and 2007, an average of 182 large ships were lost every single year. Over the 12 years, this amounts to 160 million gt.

Cases of sense-making leading to catastrophic consequences abound in other safety-critical industrial sectors too, including Defence, Petro-chemical, Nuclear, Rail and Air. The problem is not specific to maritime and is found wherever there is human activity.

## When does sense-making become a problem?

Human sense-making problems in the shipping industry arise in several ways.

Firstly, there are now many practices, procedures, technologies, rules and regulations aimed at controlling the way things are done on land and at sea. They are

well intended, but they can do the opposite of what they are meant to. This is because it is assumed that, ultimately, enough rules and technologies will have been created to cope with all situations.

For example, accident investigators and regulators typically come up with new procedures to plug the gaps exposed by the

> ## "Automation creates new human weaknesses ... and amplifies existing ones"
> Lützhöft & Dekker (2002)

latest incident. But as we have seen in this section, the situations aren't out there in the world. Instead they are created by people who are trying to make sense of their surroundings, informed by their current needs, constraints, purposes and past experiences. And each situation is new – not just because things never happened quite like this before, but because the pattern of human needs influencing each of the people involved is also unique.

Rules and technologies that are created to plug holes in previous operations tend to be either over-prescriptive or over-complicated, likely to conflict with each other and overload the people required to use them. At worst they don't apply because their creators did not (and could not) foresee the situation people are now in.

Bigger rule books and more gadgets increase uncertainty, ambiguity and complexity – resulting in greater opportunity for more interpretations of unfolding events. Automation in particular creates greater distance between people and the world around them, making them more isolated from it, and less able to notice or take effective action if things go wrong. People can be lulled into a false sense of security by confusing the reliability of technology with its robustness in dealing with novel or unexpected developments. The widely used expression 'radar-assisted collisions' refers directly to this kind of problem. Consider, for example, what happened to the *Royal Majesty*.

In 1995, the Panamanian cruise ship *Royal Majesty* ran aground east of Nantucket with 1,000 passengers aboard. At the time, she was 17 nautical miles from her planned and presumed course. There were no injuries, but repairs and lost revenues cost the company US$7 million. She was off course because, unnoticed, her GPS had been knocked into dead reckoning mode when a crew member inadvertently kicked an antenna cable loose as she was leaving Bermuda. The crew had spent the entire voyage making sense of things based on their false assumption that the GPS must be correct. Their repeated observations of the radar and the views from the bridge over 36 hours simply led them to force what they saw into what they expected to see[4].

---

[4] Lützhöft & Dekker (2002)

## Cultural differences increase the likelihood of different interpretations of the same event

A second problem is when insufficient attention is paid by shipping organisations to training in teamworking skills, communication skills and the true nature of human sense-making (eg as part of BRM, OOW, Rating, Deck and Engineering Officer progression training courses). Sense-making in the shipping industry is particularly vulnerable to differences in the ethnic cultures of crew members (see earlier panel, *How does a person's culture affect their sense-making?*).

The lack of attention in this area results in increased risk of misunderstandings arising between people who depend on each other for their safety, the integrity of the environment and, ultimately, the profitability of their employers.

Together, these two problems create a vicious circle. The more rules and technologies there are, the more technical training time is required to teach them. This reduces the time available for training in the true nature of sense-making.

In turn, this increases (or maintains the rate of) maritime accidents – which tends to lead to more rules and technologies to try to deal with them, resulting in even less time for the training that is really needed to fix the problem!

# DO's

*Puzzled by someone's behaviour?*
DO consider asking them before you act – perhaps they know something you don't!

*Need to see the world through someone else's eyes?*
If someone does something unsafe or they appear confused about something, there's a handy technique called the Five Whys? It was invented by Sakichi Toyoda and used as a key component of problem solving training at Toyota. To use it, DO ask them why they did what they did. Then why again. By the time you get to the fifth 'why', you will see where the problem really is, and understand more about the situation they believed they were in.

*Work in a culturally mixed environment?*
DO make sure you receive training in teamworking and communication skills in mixed cultures. It is vital to understand how you and your messages appear to other people, and what motivates them to behave the way they do.

*Are you a designer or equipment buyer?*
DO make sure you pay attention to training requirements and competence definitions as well as usability considerations. You also need to work with your users to understand how the new kit will change their perceptions, assumptions and, ultimately, the way they do the job. Remember that automation always fixes one problem at the expense of creating another one. You always need to pay attention to the downside.

*Are you a regulator or investigator?*
DO try to make recommendations or specify rules that make clear what needs to be achieved, without telling seafarers or shipowners how to do it.

## DON'Ts

DON'T assume other people know what you know – or that they have made the same interpretation as you. Everyone around you got here by a different route and they all have different pressures on them: they may see quite different implications and possibilities.

DON'T ignore the natural hierarchy of personal needs that everyone has. In order, they are *physiological* (eg breathing, food, drink etc), *safety* (eg personal, financial etc), *social* (eg friendship, family etc) *self-respect*, and *self-development* (eg so that people can become everything they want to be). Each level needs to be satisfied before the next level can be properly addressed.

DON'T underestimate the power of your feelings, personal circumstances, current pressures and past experience to shape how and what you pay attention to. They have a lot to do with what you decide to do next.

## Around the buoys again

The main points covered by this section are as follows.

We filter out most of the information around us.
To do this, we rely on mental filters that help us create and retain meaningful information in terms of our personal needs, self-concept, past experience, shared goals and the plausible possibilities for action.

As a result, we are always in a unique situation of our own construction. Furthermore, the filters that we use make us see the things we expect and want to see. We can only share our own situation with others to the extent that we can effectively empathise and communicate with each other.

Empathy and communication require effective training investment by the shipping industry. This is because most of us don't find it easy to challenge the meanings either we or our colleagues give to situations. This is all the more so when part of that meaning is due to differences in rank, cultural tradition and cultural difference.

## Deeper waters

This section has drawn on the following books, reports and papers:

Lewis R.D. (2006) *When Cultures Collide*, Nicholas Brealey Publishing

Lloyd's Register (2000) *World Casualty Statistics*. London: Lloyd's Register: http://www.lrfairplay.com/Maritime_data/statistics.html, (in Mar '10)

Lützhöft M.H. & Dekker S.W.A. (2002) *On Your Watch: Automation on the Bridge*. Journal of Navigation, 55(1), 83-96

MAIB (1999) *Investigation into the collision between the UK registered cargo vessel Hoo Robin and the Republic of Ireland registered cargo vessel Arklow Marsh on the River Trent on 2 March 1999*, Marine Accident Investigation Branch, Carlton House, Carlton Place, Southampton, SO15 2DZ, File 1/3/66

Maslow A. (1943) *A Theory of Human Motivation*, Psychological Review, 50, 370-396

USCG (1979) *USCGC Cuyahoga, M/V Santa Cruz II (Argentine): Collision in Chesapeake Bay on 20 Oct 1978 with loss of life, US Coast Guard Marine Board of Investigation Report and Commandant's Action*, United States Coastguard Service Report No. 16732/92368, 31 Jul 1979

RIVERDANCE
IMO 7635361

# Taking risks

## What is risk?

We live in a world of uncertainty. In the previous section on *Making sense of things* we looked at how we overcome this by imposing our sense on it. The problem is that however good our sense-making is, it can never match the complexity of the world.

As a result, the meaning that we create is always tinged with doubt. Some uncertainty always remains. Said another way, the assumptions we make and the things we do in the world all attract an element of *risk*.

Risk refers to the chance that our sense-making turns out to be inadequate to deal with the world safely and effectively.

## What affects our assessment of risk?

Our perception of risk has little to do with the actual probability of something bad happening (see panel, *Are risk and probability the same thing?*). The problem is not a matter of calculating probability – though that is difficult enough for most of us.

Just as there are a number of factors that affect the sense we make of things, so there are a number of factors affecting our assessment of the risks we take. There are three main factors that influence our sense of risk.

Here they are:

- The amount of *control* we think we have

- The amount of *value* something has for us

- The extent to which things are *familiar* to us

Let's have a look at these in a little more detail.

### Perceived control

The more control we believe we have, the less risk we believe we are taking. In the maritime industry, shore-based staff believe the risk of ship incidents is twice as great as crew members do[1]. The high degree of control a person thinks they have may be real – due to a well-calibrated sense of their own well-developed skills, together with a highly pertinent assessment of the situation they are in. At the other extreme, it may be far from the truth – due to over-confidence, lack of appreciation of missing skills or knowledge, stress or fatigue – amongst other influences. In one incident, a deckhand was washed overboard when he underestimated the amount of control he had over the conditions. He had secured himself to the vessel by crooking his arm over the pulpit rail rather than using the harness in heavy seas (see later panel, *Lucky dip*).

> ## The perception of risk has little to do with actual probability.

[1] Bailey et al (2006)



At first sight, risk seems similar to probability. Insurance Clubs calculate risk (eg of collision or loss) in terms of probability so that they can work out the premiums shipowners must pay. Insurance risk is calculated from historical data and its accuracy depends on past statistical relationships holding in the future.

However, the statistical rules of probability are very different from what drives people's perception of risk in everyday life. Consider these three possible sets of results of flipping a coin eight times (there are, of course, many such sequences of Heads and Tails – actually 256 in all).

1. HHTHTTHT
2. HHHHTTTT
3. TTTTTTTT

When asked about the probability of these sequences actually occurring, many people give the order 1, 2, 3. According to the laws of probability, however, each sequence has an identical chance of appearing. When asked the likelihood of a ninth Tail being thrown at the end of sequence 3, again many people believe it to be less likely than a Head. It is not. On each flip, there is a 50/50 chance of either a Head or a Tail.

*Confusing probability with typicality*
According to Piattelli-Palmarini (1994), the problem here is that people confuse the formal logic of *probability* with the everyday logic of *typicality*. The laws of probability work for very large numbers, but people are not sensitive to the large-scale patterns that these laws describe. Instead, people imagine that the 'balance of probability' occurs much sooner, in the smaller patterns that are more typical for us.

People do not have a naturally good grasp of probability. For a particularly powerful example of this, see the panel on the next page, *How to win a Rolls Royce*.

## How to win a Rolls Royce

In the 1960s, the TV presenter Monty Hall presented the game show *"Let's Make a Deal"* in the US. Here is a quayside version of his famous probability puzzle.

On a quayside are three identical containers. While you are busy in the cargo hold, I drive a Rolls Royce into one of them, walk out and shut the container door. When you return, I invite you to consider the three containers and guess which one contains the Rolls Royce. If you get it right, you can keep the car. There is no way you can tell which one contains the Rolls Royce, so you randomly point to one.

Next, I tell you I am going to open one of the other two containers – one which I know to be empty. If I know you have chosen the container with the car in, I will randomly choose either one of the other containers. If I know you have chosen an empty container, I will choose the other empty one. I make my choice and open it to show you it is empty. There are now two unopened containers, one of which contains the Rolls Royce and the other of which is empty. I now ask you if you would like to stay with your original choice, or whether you would like to switch to the other unopened container.

*So, how do you maximise your chance of ending up with the Rolls?*

Incredible as it may seem, the answer is always to select the other container. It will contain the car twice as often as your original choice. But how can this be? Our strong intuition says that faced with two containers, there can only be a 50/50 chance that either container conceals the car. But the laws of probability do not work that way. When there were three containers, the one you chose had a one-third chance of containing the car, and the other two combined had a two-thirds probability. If one of those is revealed to be empty, then the two-thirds probability now transfers to the remaining container. Hence, it stands a much better chance of containing the car than your original choice.

If you do swap your container, it may well be the empty one, but if we keep repeating the game, you will end up with twice as many Rolls Royces as you would if you stayed with your original choice!

## Perceived value

The more a course of action appears to support a goal that we regard as important or highly desirable, the less risky it will appear to be (or the more we will overlook the risk normally associated with it). For example, one foggy morning, the Master of a passenger ship decided to leave his berth 10 minutes before a cargo ship cleared the same channel. He was already running late and his company and his passengers were all keen to avoid further delay. After the collision that followed, 17 passengers were hospitalised (see later panel, *More haste, less speed*).

An action will also appear to be of high value if it seems the easiest way to achieve a desired goal. We are routinely attracted to short cuts for this very reason – sometimes with dire consequences (see later panel, *Tragedy so close to home*).

## Perceived familiarity

The more a circumstance or action seems familiar, the less risky it will appear to be. Complacency is a much mentioned problem in the shipping industry and is often attributed to people who allow familiarity to blunt their sensitivity to risk. For example, on a dark, but clear Baltic night, a UK container ship collided with a fishing vessel with its halogen deck lights brightly lit up. The problem was that no-one was on either bridge, with the crews well inside their zones of familiarity, engaged on other matters, (see later panel, *The lights were on, but no-*

## Anchoring in deep water

What happens when a person finds themself (metaphorically speaking) in deep or unfamiliar waters and needs to make a snap decision?

There is an effect, well known to psychologists, called 'anchoring' in which people will use one piece of information to help them with a judgment about something else – even when there is absolutely no relationship between the two.

For example, get someone to pick the number of a day in the year from 1 to 365. Then ask them to estimate the number of spoken languages in the world. Do this for several different people and you will find that the size of the first number seems to influence the size of the second.

Stage magicians sometimes use this effect to help manipulate the 'free' choice that people think they are making, without their awareness.

*one was home*). Like human error (see section on *Making mistakes*), complacency is better seen as an effect rather than a cause.

If our surroundings are familiar, we feel safer and more comfortable. If we need to take a decision that is outside our comfort zone, we will often seize upon anything from our immediate environment – even if it's unrelated. We then use this as an 'anchor' for our decision (see panel, *Anchoring in deep water*).

The important thing about these three factors is that their overall mix is determined by the person who is exposed to risk. The actual risk any one of us takes is a combination of our personal mix on the one hand and, on the other, the problems in the outside world that really do have nothing to do with us, eg metal fatigue, instrument failure, or a severe storm. It is no wonder that risk and its assessment is such a challenging topic.

Dealing with the perception of risk is not really about spotting dangers in the external world and avoiding them. It is much more about spotting weaknesses in our own assumptions about the world and managing the relationship between the world and our own imperfect knowledge of it.

Later, we will see what can be done to improve the accuracy of risk assessment. In the meantime, let's look at a tragic example of the three personal risk factors in action.

### Case study: Fatal collision in the Dover Straits[2]

On a sunny afternoon in October 2001, in clear conditions and moderate seas, the 1,009gt motor vessel *Ash* was in the Dover Strait *en route* from Denmark to Spain with a cargo of steel coils. On board were six crew as she made just over 6 knots in a south-westerly direction off Hastings. Behind her, the 4,671gt chemical tanker *Aquamarine* was in the same traffic lane, *en route* from Antwerp to Swansea. *Aquamarine* had a mixed chemical cargo and a crew of 12 on board. At more than 12 knots, she was making twice the speed of *Ash* and was overtaking most of the traffic in front of her. Traffic was bunched towards the northern edge of the lane and close passing was commonplace.

*Ash's* Master had worked on similar vessels managed by his current shipowner for about two years and had joined the ship three months before. At the time of the collision he was in his cabin resting. *Ash's* Chief Officer had worked at sea for 15 years and had joined four months earlier for his first voyage with this shipowner. At the time of the collision he was on watch alone on the bridge.

*Aquamarine's* Master had worked for his shipowner for over 20 years, although he had only joined the ship one week before the accident. He did not keep a regular bridge watch on *Aquamarine* and was in his cabin resting when the collision occurred. *Aquamarine's* Chief Officer had 20 years of sea experience, but had only joined the ship three weeks before. He had handed the watch to the Second Officer at midday and was in his cabin resting at the time of the collision, four hours later. *Aquamarine's* Second Officer also had 20 years experience, including two months experience of *Aquamarine's* sister ship. Like the Master and Chief Officer he, too, was new to *Aquamarine*, having joined its crew just a week before. At the time of the collision he was alone on the bridge.

*Ash* had been making a steady course and speed for several hours before the collision. Her Chief Officer first became aware of *Aquamarine* when she had been five miles astern. He noticed her again when *Aquamarine* was one mile astern, but thought there was no cause for concern. It was clear to him that, as the overtaking vessel, *Aquamarine* was the give way ship. Immediately before the collision he had been speaking on the telephone, and had not monitored *Aquamarine's* final approach. He did not become alert to the risk of collision with *Aquamarine* until after the first contact, and so he made no attempt to attract the attention of *Aquamarine's* watchkeeper. He was unable to move out of *Aquamarine's* path.

## How had *Aquamarine* ploughed straight into *Ash*, as if she wasn't there?

When *Aquamarine* bounced off and then struck a second time, *Ash* was holed below the waterline, flooding her cargo hold, and she began to list severely to starboard. There was no time to launch lifeboats. *Ash's* Master, by now on the bridge, gave the order for the crew to jump clear, but then fell from the bridge wing to the deck below, badly injuring himself. All six made it into the sea as *Ash* capsized and sank vertically, bow first. All but one were recovered by *Aquamarine's* lifeboat. *Ash's* Master was found floating face down and despite prolonged attempts to resuscitate him on the scrambled rescue helicopter and ashore, he was later pronounced dead.

How had *Aquamarine* ploughed straight into *Ash*, in broad daylight – almost as if she wasn't there?

The subsequent investigation showed that neither alcohol nor fatigue had played a part. If we look closely, however, we can see all three risk-influencing factors at work.

[2] Based on MAIB (2003) with further interpretation by the authors

### Perceived control

*Aquamarine* was equipped with a modern Integrated Bridge System (IBS), which included the ability to use track control, a system that *Aquamarine's* Master and officers had found to be very useful, and was in use at the time of the accident. In track control mode, the autopilot maintains the vessel precisely on a pre-determined track. If a deviation from the track becomes necessary, eg for collision avoidance, the watchkeeper can take control immediately by simply operating the tiller, before allowing the system to take the vessel back to the pre-determined course. The track control system is easy to operate and produces a high degree of perceived control.

### Perceived value

In the days before GPS, navigators would often steer the ship after an avoidance manoeuvre parallel to the original track until the next waypoint. With the track control system, however, it is easier to allow it to return the vessel to the original planned track automatically. While track control systems have functions that enable a new course to the next waypoint to be programmed, many navigators are not adept at using them. On *Aquamarine*, the Second Officer had received no formal training in the operation of the track control system. His limited experience meant that simply letting the system get the ship back on the right course was a valuable facility because it required minimal effort and apparently minimised the chance of error.

### Perceived familiarity

Using the track control system, *Aquamarine* was catching and overtaking the ships ahead of her in a busy shipping lane. Only an hour or so before the collision with *Ash*, the Second Officer had allowed *Aquamarine* to auto-revert to her original track after passing another ship, even though the reverted course meant she had then passed a third ship at a distance of only 0.15 mile. Close passing seemed familiar, normal and safe. The detail of track control operation was not understood, but a context of perceived familiarity had developed on the bridge of *Aquamarine* during the afternoon, as well as, no doubt, in the previous days of its routine use.

In *Aquamarine's* case, it is likely that the operation of these factors helped to make people less capable of maintaining an appropriate sensitivity to the real risks. As a result, it was easy to overlook *Ash* on radar, partially obscured as she was by the heading marker on the radar screen, for over an hour before the collision. Despite the fact that the watchkeeper was on the bridge and actively engaged in his task, these factors also meant that *Ash's* visual aspect would be overlooked. Her stern was low in the water and, combined with her blue hull and white superstructure, she simply blended with the surrounding seascape.

### How can people become better attuned to risk?

First, it is important to realise that risk can't be eliminated altogether. As we have explained in this section, risk is a consequence of the uncertainty of the world around us.

Second, even if it was possible in principle, people wouldn't agree to it in practice. People need risk to provide excitement and to avert boredom. If there is not enough risk present, people make their actions riskier to compensate. There is evidence that while people differ in the amount of risk to which they will expose themselves, they all alter their behaviour to maintain the amount of risk with which they feel comfortable. This is why the risk reductions offered by road safety improvements such as seat belts, air bags, ABS and vehicle crumple zones result in people driving faster and closer. What they have not done is produce an overall reduction in road accidents.

So, it is not risk elimination that we should seek, but rather, give people the means to become more accurately aware of risk – in both their own behaviour and the behaviour of their colleagues. This comes down to appropriate training in the human perception of risk and the factors that influence it.

## More haste, less speed

On a winter's morning in the River Clyde, a 100gt chartered passenger ship, with 44 people on board, left her berth in worsening visibility. The highly experienced skipper was given the option of waiting 10 minutes for a 2500gt container ship to pass, giving him a clear channel in the fog. But his chartered vessel was already running 30 minutes late and the skipper felt he had the necessary control and familiarity with his surroundings. So he took the course of action that he felt provided the best value to his company and his charter passengers. In doing so, his sensitivity to risk was substantially reduced.

A few minutes later, in thick fog, the passenger ship and the cargo ship lost each other in the 'sunspots' at the centre of their respective radar screens. When the passenger vessel hit the cargo ship's starboard side, many of her passengers lost their footing and were thrown against tables, chairs, bulkheads and each other. Unsecured fittings caused further injuries and 17 people were hospitalised, one in a serious condition.

## Lucky dip

In gale force winds and 1.5-metre seas, a pilot launch drew alongside a general cargo ship to disembark the Pilot. The Pilot informed the pilot launch that due to the conditions, he needed to disembark as quickly as possible. This led to two short cuts. First, the launch deckhand went forward to steady the pilot ladder early – before the Pilot was sighted. Second, the deckhand relied on securing his own safety by simply wrapping his arm round the pulpit rail rather than taking time to deploy a harness.

The launch's bow suddenly dipped into a trough and shipped a lot of water. The deckhand was washed overboard and was lucky to be recovered safely only six minutes later by a second pilot launch.

The deckhand was a victim of overestimating the amount of control he had over the conditions and paying too much attention to his own efficiency in trying to provide value. He was also (no doubt) beguiled by the times he had successfully performed this task on previous occasions. The result was a substantially reduced understanding of the true level of risk he was taking, and he was fortunate to be able to return to work the next day.

Stories of people underestimating risk are legion.

Some have dreadful consequences.

*More haste, less speed*, based on MAIB Report 40/2001, Collision between *Nordsee* and *Poole Scene* in the River Clyde, Dec 2000
*Lucky Dip*, based on Case 7, MAIB Safety Digest 1/2007
*The lights were on, but no-one was home*, based on Case 10, MAIB Safety Digest 1/2007
*Tragedy so close to home*, based on Case 14, MAIB Safety Digest 1/2007

All with further interpretation by the authors.

## The lights were on, but no-one was home

In the middle of a clear Baltic night, a UK container ship approached a fishing vessel that was drifting between hauls. At the time of the resulting collision, there was no-one on either bridge. The Master of the container ship was in the bridge toilet and had felt he remained in sufficient control by leaving the door ajar so that he was in earshot of any VHF calls from other vessels. Such was his sense of control that he did not feel it necessary to set alarms on his radar for either auto acquisition or closest point of approach.

Meanwhile the entire crew of the fishing vessel were eating dinner together in their mess room. The Master felt he had exercised sufficient control by switching on their halogen deck lights, thereby making the vessel a highly visible beacon. Both Masters' control assumptions relied on being sighted by the other and overlooked the risk these assumptions produced. The ice-strengthened bow of the container ship seriously damaged the fishing vessel, which was only just able to limp into harbour.

## Tragedy so close to home

A cable-laying vessel was returning to port after a long voyage and everyone on board was keen to get home. Unfortunately, this was not to be for an experienced member of the crew. The plan was to embark a Pilot at 06.00 and berth at 08.00. But unexpected tide conditions forced a choice between either an earlier Pilot or a wait for the next tide. Not surprisingly, the earlier time was chosen.

Rigging the pilot ladder was a four-man task, but when the earlier time came, one of the ABs had not appeared, since he had not been told of the new plan. One AB went to rouse the other one, and – with the Pilot embarkation deadline approaching – the four-man task was attempted by the remaining two, the Bosun and the Bosun's Mate. As the ladder was being adjusted for height, the Bosun lost his balance and fell overboard. Although he was recovered from the water just nine minutes later and received good medical attention, he was pronounced dead on arrival at hospital 43 minutes after the accident.

The crew were victims of reduced sensitivity to risk due to overestimating their perceived control, as well as being seduced by the perceived value of getting home as soon as possible.

## DO's

DO be suspicious if things seem under control, on track, familiar, comfortable, quiet and safe. You are almost certainly missing something.

DO try to arrange training in the human perception of risk as part of your technical training for you and your team. You are unlikely to get the necessary insight into risk taking without it, and it will also help avert the development of complacency.

*Are you a designer or equipment buyer?*
DO establish how the new kit will affect the risk awareness and risk management strategies of their users. Will they get bored? How are they likely to compensate for reduced risk by increasing it elsewhere? Will their original skills fade dangerously?

## DON'Ts

DON'T confuse qualifications with experience. People cannot become properly aware of the risks of their working environment unless they have been directly exposed to it for a suitably long period, mentored by colleagues who are already aware of those risks. If people are promoted without the relevant experience, they will underestimate the risks they take as well as all those in their charge, exposing themselves, their colleagues, their companies and the environment to danger and potentially huge costs.

DON'T confuse a person's rank with the status of their information. It's the person with the relevant information and experience who is often best placed to raise a concern. The higher a person's rank, the greater the responsibility they have to ensure that those with the relevant knowledge are heard. This responsibility is much easier to carry if an organisation has been able to develop a 'just culture' – see section on *Making mistakes*.

## Around the buoys again

The main points covered by this section are as follows.

Our perception of risk is not a matter of calculating probability. Probability is concerned with statistical patterns which people do not find easy to understand.

Risk refers to the chance that a person's sense-making is insufficient to deal with the world safely and effectively.

Risk cannot be eliminated. It is always present because the world is always uncertain. Uncertainty arises as a result of information which is missing, unreliable, ambiguous or complex.

Our perception of risk keeps changing and is influenced by the degree to which we feel in control, the amount of value a course of action has for us, and the degree of familiarity we feel.

Most of us need risk. Without it, we become bored and inattentive. If there is not enough, we create it by behaving in a riskier way.

Complacency is better understood as the result of a person's badly calibrated sense of risk, rather than as a fundamental cause of incidents.

We need better insight into our own risk-taking so that we can maintain it at a level that is appropriate to the real levels of control we have.

## Deeper waters

This section has drawn on the following books, reports and papers:

Bailey N., Ellis N. & Sampson H. (2006) *Perceptions of Risk in the Maritime Industry*, Seafarers International Research Institute (SIRC)

MAIB (2003a) *Report on the investigation on the collision between mv Ash and mv Dutch Aquamarine in the SW lane of the Dover Strait TSS with the loss of one life, 9 October 2001*, Marine Accident Investigation Branch, First Floor, Carlton House, Carlton Place, Southampton, UK, SO15 2DZ, Report No 7/2003, March 2003

Piattelli-Palmarini M. (1994) *Inevitable illusions: how mistakes of reason rule our minds*, John Wiley & Sons Inc

Slovic P. (2000) *The perception of risk*, Earthscan Publications Ltd

Sprent P. (1988) *Taking risks: the science of uncertainty*, Penguin Books

# Making decisions

## How do people make decisions?

At first sight, the answer seems rather straightforward. Let's say you want to buy a new TV. You might collect as much information about the available products as possible, compare each of them with your needs, wishes and budget, and home in on the product that best fits your criteria. This approach is known as *rational decision making*. In its purest form, it depends on:

- Having complete information about all the alternatives
- Being able to distinguish and understand all the relevant differences between the alternatives
- Using comprehensive criteria – that will be relevant throughout the life of the decision's consequences – for rank ordering all the alternatives
- Having the time to do all of the above

In reality, even the decision to buy a TV usually falls short of these characteristics. We may be persuaded by advertising, friendly advice, or our own experience to consider only one or two brands. We may have to make assumptions about which technology will be most future-proof, eg HD vs Blu-ray. We may not understand the differences between the various component technologies on offer, eg LCD vs Plasma. Most significantly, we usually do not have the time for an exhaustive investigation of all the alternatives.

In our working lives, we are faced with two problems that make fully rational decision making impossible.

First, the practicalities of our ongoing tasks mean that we do not have time to do it. Instead we must rely on an alternative approach which produces the best decisions using the available information in the available time. Second, we live in an uncertain world where complete information is never available.

## Available time

The time available for us to think and act is a major determinant of the decisions we make. Experienced people often appear to have more time, resulting in smoother performance. Experienced people who are also experts perform not only more smoothly in the available time, but also perform more effectively and more safely over time.

## Available information

As you can see from the section on *Making sense of things*, we only use a fraction of the information that is available to us: perception involves an active search for information whose relevance is determined by a series of mental filters.

If people in operational settings such as seafaring do not have either the time or the information to make purely rational decisions, what are they doing?

> **People's decisions are a trade-off between the available information and the available time**

## *Efficiency versus thoroughness*

Recent analysis[1] shows that the smooth flow of decisions that people make throughout their working day depends on them making a continuous series of trade-offs between efficiency and thoroughness.

Efficiency increases when people spend less time and effort in thinking, and more time and effort in acting. When this balance is reversed, thoroughness increases at the expense of efficiency.

If safety and quality are paramount to an organisation or the individuals within it, thoroughness will tend to be favoured by individual decision makers. If production targets and output are emphasised, then efficiency will be favoured.

In practice, most organisations must be both safety conscious and profitable. However, the fact that efficiency and thoroughness are trade-offs means that it is impossible to maximise both at the same time. This tension is the source of a huge organisational problem.

Simply stated, the problem is that every decision made is always a compromise. The amount of unnecessary risk – either to profits or to safety – signified by a particular decision depends on the extent to which

[1] Hollnagel (2009)

the decision maker is accurately aware of the real (not just perceived) risks they are dealing with. Appropriate thoroughness is produced by training, mentoring, and properly debriefed job experience, acquired over time. Such training and experience also produces a natural efficiency of performance that arises from expertise and good judgment. A less natural kind of efficiency arises when organisational requirements to be profitable and competitive start to influence decision making against an individual's better judgment.

If we are not sufficiently trained or, alternatively, if we perceive organisational expectations as too demanding, then the risks we take in our decision making will increase. Furthermore, we and our colleagues will often not know the extent of this increased risk until the ill-founded assumptions or undue pressures that underlie our decisions are catastrophically tested.

Later in this section there is a summary of the key principles – both individual and organisational – that people use to make trade-offs between efficiency and thoroughness. Before that, here are some of these trade-offs in action.

## Case study: The day that efficiency led to tragedy[2]

An LNG tanker was berthed for repairs to her main boilers. The work was being carried out by a well-established boiler repair contractor who was familiar with the vessel. As the repairs neared completion, the repairer subcontracted a chemical cleaning expert, who was well known to them, to carry out a chemical clean of the internal surfaces of the boilers.

The expert did not have a method statement or any risk assessments to support his work, and none was asked for. There was a blind acceptance that he was the expert, and those on site, including the ship's engineers, had virtually no interaction with him.

Following a successful pressure test, the starboard boiler was cleaned of oils and greases using a proprietary alkaline cleaner. This went without incident and was completed the following day. Meanwhile, the ship managers arranged for a second subcontractor, another chemical cleaning expert, to oversee the chemical clean on their behalf. Although this was not unusual for high-value contracts, neither the contractor, nor the first expert was aware of his impending arrival.

At 08.00 on the day of the chemical clean, the water was heated and circulated around the boiler. By 13.00 the water was at 57°C, and the second expert, worried that the continued heating would make the inhibitor ineffective, recommended that the heating steam be turned off. By mid afternoon 800kg of the acid inhibitor had been added to the water/acid mixing tank. At 17.00 tests were carried out which confirmed that the inhibitor was still active.

By 21.00 things had rapidly changed. Tests indicated that the boiler steel was being attacked by the acid. The first expert was rather sceptical about the interpretation of the test results because he had expected to circulate the water/acid mixture

Examining the boiler that exploded

a little longer. However, he agreed to stop the circulation and pumped the mixture into a shore-side bowser. In the meantime, he asked the prime repair contractor to arrange for the door of the starboard boiler steam drum to be opened so that the internal surfaces of the boiler could be inspected.

At 21.45 the steam drum door was opened. There was a noticeable suction as the seal was broken. Fifteen minutes later both of the cleaning experts approached the steam drum door. No tests were conducted to check the steam drum atmosphere for either toxic or flammable gases. The first expert picked up a nearby halogen lamp and placed it just inside the steam drum. The second expert saw a small spark, and an explosion immediately followed. The first expert was thrown backwards about 4.5 metres. He was found unconscious with a number of fractures and severe burns. Sadly he failed to recover from his injuries and died nine days later. The second expert was also burned, but less severely.

All the evidence points to an accumulation of hydrogen gas in the steam drum, which developed during the cleaning procedure. As the steam drum door was opened, the air combined with the hydrogen to create a mixture that was within the hydrogen's wide explosive limits. As the first expert introduced the unprotected halogen lamp, it ignited the mixture, causing the explosion.

What were the efficiency-thoroughness trade-offs here? This was a high-value contract in which time was money, both in terms of direct repair costs and indirect ship downtime costs. In this context:

- It was more efficient for the ship's crew to leave things to the experts.

- It was more efficient to stop heating the inhibiting mixture rather than risk reducing its inhibiting power and having to start all over again.

- It was more efficient to open up the steam drum as early as possible to inspect the results of the inhibiting mixture.

- It was more efficient to reach for the nearest light source, so making the inspection easier.

- It was more efficient for one expert to go along with the procedure of another and allow the steam drum to be opened without the safety checks.

And all these efficiencies reduced the thoroughness that was actually required to avert the death and serious injury that resulted.

## What draws us towards efficient decisions?

Generally speaking, we all want to make decisions that allow us to carry out a stream of work as efficiently as possible. Usually this is because we want to maximise the time available for the next thing we have to deal with – whether this is a planned activity or because we need to plan for the unexpected.

The amount of training and properly managed experience we have had will help us apply due care and attention (ie thoroughness). Inappropriate organisational pressure will tend to decrease such diligence. We might expect this to be a particular pro r anyone who has not received the right training and experience. But as the case of the chemical cleaning contractors shows, expertise is no protection.

Why might this be? The panel, *The Behavioural Rule Book*, shows the practical rules that seem to guide people in the work place. It is notable that all these behavioural rules are biased towards efficiency. There are a few behavioural rules that bias our decision making the other way, towards thoroughness. For example, *'If a job's worth doing, it's worth doing well'* or *'Don't spoil the ship for a ha'p'orth of tar.'* However, such rules seem to belong to an earlier world where time was not as important.

If we consider the tragic case of the exploding boiler again, it is possible to spot several of these behavioural rules at work. These include (1), (2), (7), (9) and (10) from the panel.

In the following case, which also ended in tragedy, a different combination of behavioural rules was at work.

## Case study: Death on *Saga Rose*[3]

On 11 June 2008, a motorman found an experienced petty officer, who was also a close friend, lying at the bottom of a ballast tank on board the cruise ship *Saga Rose* while the ship was visiting Southampton, UK. The petty officer was the vessel's Second Bosun, who had been sent to the tank to determine whether it contained fresh or salt water. The motorman raised the alarm and then returned to the scene and entered the tank to help the petty officer. The motorman then also collapsed. The onboard emergency response team quickly arrived with breathing apparatus, and the local emergency services were called to assist. The motorman was successfully revived and evacuated from the tank, but the Second Bosun died before he could be recovered.

He had been instructed to test the water in the tank on the assumption that the tank was full and the water was within easy reach from outside the tank. As a result, a permit to work was not deemed necessary. However, the tank contained only a small amount of water and the Second Bosun entered it despite being aware of, and practised in, the vessel's procedures for entering enclosed spaces. But the tank contained insufficient oxygen to sustain human life due to steel corrosion and he collapsed almost immediately.

What behavioural rules were in use here (see earlier panel, *The Behavioural Rule Book*)? Firstly, the efficiency of assuming the tank was full of water averted the need for a permit to work procedure to be initiated (Rule 2).

Secondly, the efficiency of testing the water in the tank by entering it against laid-down safety procedures proved fatal for the Second Bosun (Rule 1).

Thirdly, after discovering his friend, the efficiency of action that appeared to be demanded by the emergency situation nearly proved fatal for the motorman (Rule 7). Clearly, the effect of the stress and emotion of the moment played its part here as well, and we will return to this in the section on *Getting tired and stressed*.

## How does culture influence decision making?

Our use of behavioural rules in the work place is influenced by two different sets of cultural issues. The first of these relates to differences due to a person's cultural background – see the panel, *How does a person's culture affect their sense-making?* in the section *Making sense of things*.

A person's cultural origins may make them more or less likely to break with laid-down procedures, defer to expertise, or more generally, prefer efficiency to thoroughness (or *vice versa*).

A person's ethnicity may also make them more or less sensitive to the demands of the second set of cultural issues – the organisational culture in which the decision makers are embedded. The panel, *How does organisational culture influence decision making?*, describes some of the main efficiency-thoroughness trade-offs that work at cultural levels within organisations.

### Does all this help explain why we break rules?

Yes. At work we are embedded in organisational cultures, which are dominated by time and cost. It is in this context that we make trade-offs between efficiency and thoroughness, guided by whatever training and experience we have had. When people knowingly break company rules, they usually do so to improve the efficiency of their own work, or that of their colleagues.

In fact rule-breaking is quite widespread. For example, ship inspectors often find that in some less responsible companies, the crew may complete ship's duty hour logs to comply with the law or company policy rather than to record actual hours worked. More generally, you only have to consider what happens in organisations when a workforce decides to 'work to rule'. In such circumstances, the viability of some companies can be threatened quite quickly. How would yours do?

For more information on this topic, see the panel, *Why do people break rules?*

# People usually break rules to make work more efficient.

## What's different about expert decision making?

Decision makers are dependent on their training and experience for the quality of their decisions. In particular, in making decisions, lots of relevant experience allows us to be better tuned to the real risks of the situation we think we are in (see section on *Making sense of things*). But exactly how are expert decision makers better tuned than novices?

A large amount of research points to two main ways in which experts and novices differ:

- The first of these is the accuracy of the mental picture of what's going on – and what can happen next. This is often referred to as *situational awareness*.

- The second is the directness with which experts are able to arrive at good decisions – often under extreme time pressure. This depends on *situational familiarity*.

### Situational awareness

Good situational awareness depends on three levels of mental activity – all of which take place simultaneously, and all of which are subject to the active mental filters described in the section on *Making sense of things*.

These three levels are *perception*, *comprehension* and *projection*[4].

---

[4] Following Endsley (1999)



Breaking a rule that is part of company policy or published in the professional rule book often involves a deliberate and knowing act by the violater. Rule-breaking is a major cause of accidents.

Sometimes, such violations are clear breaches of law or international protocol – for example discharge of pollutants at sea or deliberate misuse of shipping lanes. However, usually when a rule is violated, it is in the name of getting the job done more efficiently rather than for any sinister reason.

*So, how do violations arise?* There are three principle ways:

- When a person attempts to solve a novel, but pressing, problem using limited knowledge and experience, rather than stopping the job and seeking advice.

- When a person takes a short-cut or creates a work-around. Such practices often become routine, passed from person to person and are organisationally tolerated because they contribute so much to efficiency. Such toleration sends mixed messages to people about the status of the rule book and the true position of management. When something goes wrong, it is often the short-cut takers and maybe those who turned a blind eye who find themselves the subject of the disciplinary enquiry, rather than the senior managers whose policies created the need for the short-cut in the first place.

- When a person's supervision is ineffective. In turn, this can:

   › allow a person to break rules unchecked, eg in an ill-judged attempt to prove to their fellow crew members that they are highly skilled

   › allow complacency to develop when long periods of unsupervised rule breaking do not result in adverse incidents

   › allow rule breaking to get worse (ie more frequent and/or more extreme) due to ill-defined accountabilities.

## Perception

In making decisions we must be able to pick out all the pieces of information in our environment that are relevant to our goals. Some of these may be very subtle, such as small changes over time in what an instrument says or the sea state. Some may rely on memory, such as what someone told us on watch handover. And some will be very obvious, such as a bridge alarm. In complex situations, many disparate information sources may be relevant and they all may be simultaneously competing for our attention. They may also be hidden away, requiring a deliberate search to find them.

## Comprehension

However disparate or numerous the relevant individual information elements are, in making decisions we must be able to integrate them in a way which allows us to form a coherent picture of what is going on around us. It is here that we establish the meaning, significance and priority of the information relevant to our goals. For example, if a chief engineer sees warning lights and hears unusual engine noises while under assisted tow in a restricted channel, the extent of the problem must be quickly evaluated to work out the implications for the ship and the accompanying tugs.

## Projection

Understanding the current picture is not enough for full situational awareness. Expert decision makers must also be able to project their understanding into the future. This enables them to make the decision they must take now to create the best options in the future. Projection requires us to have good mental models of the dynamic relationships between the relevant parts of our environment over time. Experts focus a lot on creating their own futures via present decisions. In turn, these decisions are formed out of their comprehension of the likely interactions of all the elements they deem both relevant and important.

Good situation awareness takes a lot of mental immersion in the task, exposure to many task variations over time, and much practice and feedback in trying to deal with those variations (see panel, *How long does it take to become an expert?*).

### Situational familiarity

Throughout the 1970s and early 1980s the US Government spent millions of dollars on decision making research. The results were used to build a series of expensive decision making aids for military commanders. But they didn't work and no-one used them[5].

---

[5] As reported by the US Army Research Institute to Klein (1999)

> **Good situation awareness requires experts to see the future.**



Ericsson (2006) says it takes 10 years or around 10,000 hours of deliberate practice to become an expert. This is a consistent answer from a great deal of research in a variety of complex decision making areas. Furthermore, it has little to do with innate 'giftedness' – even in specialist human skill areas like golf or chess.

The 10 years of deliberate practice required for a person to become an expert in golf, a musical instrument, diagnostic medicine, leadership, or a ship's Master, involves constantly engaging with tasks just beyond current levels of performance and comfort. It also involves the guidance of teachers and coaches who not only provide trainees with the feedback they need, but who can teach a person how to become their own coach. Experts are not only expert in their technical area, but have also learned how to learn (see section on *Learning and developing*).

*Experience does not equal expertise*
Expertise does not follow directly from experience. A lookout cannot acquire a Master's knowledge and skills simply by spending 10 years on the bridge. Similarly, a Master's expertise will remain very narrow if they only practise what they know. Deliberate practice is a sustained, structured engagement with scenarios that are not familiar. There are no short-cuts to this process.

*A structure for assisting seafarer development can help*
However, the process can be assisted. For example, in 2005 Teekay Marine Services launched SCOPE (Seafarer Competence for Operational Excellence), a company-specific competency management system for all its seafarers – both officers and ratings. In a similar but more restricted vein, Intertanko developed TOTS (Tanker Officer Training Standards) in 2008, an industry standard for competencies that reconciles 'time in rank' and 'time with company' criteria for officers. SIGGTO (Society of International Gas Tanker & Terminal Operators) has progressed things by specifying competency requirements embracing the ship/shore interface.

While structure helps, it is only after the requisite amount of deliberate practice that people can achieve the levels of situational awareness and familiarity that allow the smooth, effortless and competent flow of true expert performance in a variety of settings.

Then in 1984, a new approach was tried[6], and the whole area was transformed with insight and understanding. The key was changing the question from *'How do experts make decisions?'* to *'How do they do it under time pressure?'*

The new research began with the emergency services and found that expert decision makers in real life simply did not generate options, consider alternatives, make choices, or calculate probabilities. Rather they use their experience to makes sense of what they face, 'home in' on the relevant information, rapidly project a course of action into the future to check for hitches, and act – all in one smooth mental movement.

Experts try to recognise important elements of the current situation from previous experience. For example, a fire chief called to an apartment fire noticed billboards on the roof and remembered a previous case when their supports caught fire, sending the boards crashing down on the crowds below. He moved the onlookers back and saved many lives on this new occasion.

If experts are faced with a novel situation, they might borrow an idea or plan from another set of circumstances in their experience that was similar in some way. For example, recently in the UK a light aircraft pilot with nowhere to land survived an engine failure

**It takes 10 years to become an expert – and there are no short-cuts.**

by flaring his plane into a stall and landing in the tops of trees. He later reported that he got the idea from a fictional Biggles[7] story he had read years before!

Whether faced with routine or novel problems, expert decision makers spend time mentally running through their plan for the current situation, projecting a story into the future, altering details as they go, until they can see the outcome they want. They then act. As a result, their experience of the decision process is a relatively smooth, direct and continuous stream of thought, driven by a recognition of similarities between the current situation and their previous experience.

For expert decision makers, it is usually obvious what to do. For non-experts, it is hardly ever obvious. If time permits, they must rely on their knowledge of the rule book, or more likely where to find it so they can look up the relevant procedure. Very often, however, there is little time for this. If they cannot consult with a mentor, they will do whatever makes the most sense based on their limited experience (see the section, *Making sense of things*).



---

[6] Pioneered by Klein and his colleagues – see Klein (1999)

[7] A series of stories by Captain W.E. Johns, published in the 1930s, about the adventures of Biggles, a fictional British First World War pilot.

## DO's

DO recognise that everyone in the organisation constantly pursues a line between efficiency and thoroughness. If people are insufficiently trained or experienced to know when their behaviour crosses this line into unsafe levels of thoroughness, the organisation is taking a huge, uncalculated risk.

DO support investment in training and competency verification programmes (such as TOTS, SCOPE and SIGGTO) that support deliberate structured practice, apprenticeship and coaching/ mentoring in the workplace. These types of programmes are highly effective in creating the right balance between efficiency and thoroughness.

DO find ways to motivate and retain expert staff following the 10 years or so of investment necessary to bring about their expertise. It is now that they are expert that the organisation needs them!

## DONT's

DON'T send mixed messages to the workforce in which some insist on safety, while others tacitly require rule breaking to get the job done. Rule breaking is a major cause of accidents and cost.

DON'T assume that there are short-cuts to expertise in complex, knowledge-based skills such as seafaring. It takes 10 years of structured, guided experience in the job across a wide variety of scenarios and settings.

## Around the buoys again

The main points covered by this section are as follows.

We make decisions that tend to favour efficiency of action over thoroughness.

Our motivation for efficiency comes from two sources:

- First, we usually have several things to achieve in a finite timescale. Furthermore, in a world that is essentially uncertain, we try to ensure we will have enough time to deal with whatever our experience tells us could arise in the immediate future.

- Second, the organisations we work for tend to operate policies which emphasise efficiency over thoroughness – even when they might declare the opposite.

The emphasis that both individuals and whole organisations place on efficiency over thoroughness inevitably means that rule breaking is commonplace.

In making decisions, we differ in terms of the amount of situational awareness we have and the amount of situational familiarity we can recognise.

Expert decision making under time pressure involves a smooth, continuous mental flow in which there is a rapid appreciation of the important features of the environment and rapid recognition of similar circumstances from previous experience.

There is also rapid construction of an efficient plan that is accurately assessed as sufficiently thorough to lead to a clearly understood goal.

Expert decision making requires 10 years of deliberate practice, ie sustained, structured engagement with a wide range of scenarios, conditions and challenges.

There are no known short-cuts to the 10 years of deliberate practice that expertise requires for proper development. However, recent initiatives in the shipping industry such as TOTS, SCOPE and SIGGTO have made significant headway in providing structure and verification for seafaring experience.

## Deeper waters

This section has drawn on the following books, reports and papers:

Endsley M. (1999) *Situation Awareness In Aviation Systems*, in Garland D.J., Wise J.A. & Hopkin V.D. (Eds), Handbook of Aviation Human Factors, Mahwah, NJ: Lawrence Erlbaum Associates

Ericsson K.A. (2006) *The Cambridge Handbook of Expertise and Expert Performance*, Cambridge University Press

Flin R., O'Connor P. & Crichton M. (2008) *Safety at the Sharp End: A Guide to Non-Technical Skills*, Ashgate Publishing Ltd

Hollnagel E. (2009) *The ETTO Principle: Efficiency - Thoroughness Trade-Off: Why Things That Go Right Sometimes Go Wrong*, Ashgate Publishing Ltd

Klein G. (1999) *Sources of power: How people make decisions*, The MIT Press

MAIB (2008) *Part 1 - Merchant Vessels, Case 7: Main Boiler Chemical Clean Ends in Fatal Explosion*, Safety Digest 2/2008, http://www.maib.gov.uk/publications/safety_digests/2008/safetydigest_2_2008.cfm (in Mar '10)

MAIB (2009a) *Investigation Report on the Saga Rose (synopsis), Report No. 1/2009, 6 Jan 2009*; http://www.maib.gov.uk/publications/investigation_reports/2009/saga_rose.cfm (in Mar '10)

# Making mistakes

## What's the problem?

The problem is not that we make mistakes. It is normal for people – including experts – to do so. After all, it is in noticing the difference between the behaviour we want and the behaviour that we get that we are able to learn and refine our decisions and actions (see section on *Learning and developing*).

The real problem in safety-critical industries like seafaring is that some mistakes have such serious consequences that they need to be caught before they have a chance to develop into disasters. Most of the time, seafarers catch their own (and each other's) mistakes quite successfully. However, sometimes they don't and because of the nature of what they do, the results can be very serious.

It is widely reported that human error continues to be responsible for most maritime and offshore casualties. This high percentage translates into very large human losses, whether measured in lost profits, written-off investments, failed companies, ruined careers or the human misery of those affected (see panel, *2008 – an exceptionally disastrous year (or not)?*).

## What kinds of mistakes do we make?

There are three main sorts of activity in which we make mistakes[1]:

---

[1] Rasmussen (1979), Reason (1990)

---

### 2008 – an exceptionally disastrous year (or not)?

Despite the vast amount of knowledge, communications and advanced technology now available, 2008 was one of the worst yet for preventing mistakes from unfurling into full-blown catastrophes.

In 2008, the insurance company Swiss Re defined a maritime disaster as involving a claim of at least US$17.2m or with an economic impact in excess of US$85.4m.

- In 2008, 135 vessels of 100gt or above were lost – nearly three per week – representing nearly half a million tonnes (gt). Of these, 41 were maritime disasters as defined by Swiss Re.

- These 41 maritime disasters – nearly one per week – included five freighters and 32 passenger ships. They accounted for nearly a quarter of all man-made disasters for the year.

- In 2008, 1,600 people died or went missing due to maritime disasters.

- In 2008, insurers paid out US$548m for maritime casualties.

- In 2008, more than three times as many people lost their lives at sea compared with 2007.

- Around 150 people lose their lives on general cargo ships every year. This number has barely changed in the last six years.

*Sources: Swiss Re (2009), Lloyds Register (2008) and Bailey (2007)*

---

- **Skill-based activity** – where we are well practised in what we do. Here, because we can work without thinking too much about it, we can find ourselves doing something familiar (eg operating a well-used panel switch) when we should be doing something else (eg operating a less frequently used, but adjacent, panel switch). Or else, we can suffer a memory lapse (eg we suddenly forget what we were going to do next).

- **Rule-based activity** – where we have more conscious involvement with the task, and need to apply rules and procedures to what we are seeing and doing. Here, we can make a mistake by failing to apply a rule correctly, or at all (eg assuming that give-way vessels will always give way, or not realising we ourselves are the give-way vessel).

- **Knowledge-based activity** – where we must have even more conscious involvement with our task (eg where we are attending a fire and must make decisions in novel circumstances). Here, the kind of mistakes we make are often to do with the way we make sense of the situation (see section on *Making sense of things*). Decisions based on wrong interpretations of complicated or ambiguous information are usually the result of insufficient training or experience, or bad communications.

## What factors make mistakes more likely?

There are a number of factors that increase the likelihood of mistakes. Some of these factors operate at an individual level, while others are organisational.

### Individual influences on mistake-making

- **Inadequate rest or high stress levels** Fatigue and stress reduce attention, concentration and response times (see section on *Getting tired and stressed*)

- **Insufficient training and experience** Poor training or lack of experience may result in attempting to do tasks with insufficient knowledge ('a little knowledge is a dangerous thing') or else a failure to prevent a dangerous situation developing (see section on *Learning and developing*). Lack of investment in training and structured experience also contributes to a poor safety culture by sending strong signals to the workforce that they are not valued.

- **Inadequate communications**
Successful communication is not simply a matter of transmitting messages clearly. It entails empathy on the part of the messenger to assure the listener's readiness to hear, and active listening on the part of the hearer (see section on *Communicating with others*). Much communication depends on both parties' ability to make sense of the situation they share (see section on *Making sense of things*).

## *Organisational influences on mistake making*

- **Inadequate time** If there is not enough time to get everything done, we look for ways to be more efficient at the expense of thoroughness (see section on *Making decisions*). We are also likely to experience high workload levels, which increases stress levels and accelerates fatigue (see section on *Getting tired and stressed*)

- **Inadequate design** Poor design of equipment, user controls and interfaces, or work procedures, increases workload, response times, fatigue and stress levels (see section on *Getting tired and stressed*). It may also promote the invention and use of dangerous short-cuts (see sections on *Taking risks* and *Making decisions*).



- **Inadequate staffing** If the numbers of people fall short of what is required to carry out a task, then workload, fatigue, stress levels and sickness are increased (see section on *Getting tired and stressed*), short-cuts are taken (see sections on *Taking risks* and *Making decisions*), and the safety culture is compromised by demotivation, low morale and absenteeism. Management efficiencies (in the form of staff cuts) often result in unsafe working efficiencies (in the form of short-cuts), a decrease in thoroughness and an increase in the number of mistakes – all made worse due to fewer people having less time to prevent those mistakes developing into something worse.

- **Inadequate safety culture** The most influential source of a good safety culture is the seriousness with which senior management approaches it via training, staff investment and the implementation of work processes that accommodate the time that safe practices take. Workforce mistakes increase not just because of the absence of this investment, but also because of the meaning people attach to the absence of the investment by their senior management.

Unfortunately, these same factors also increase the likelihood that any mistakes will lead to serious consequences. This is because the factors also interfere with the ability to recover from mistakes once made. For example, the same fatigue that prevents a watchkeeper spotting a collision course can also interfere with their subsequent response to the emergency situation that develops.

Often, the factors help a series of mistakes combine to make a bad situation even worse. For example, a design flaw in an instrument panel made years before might combine with an engineer's tiredness, their pre-occupation over difficult personal circumstances, and their insufficient training with the panel to produce the selection of the wrong setting, or an incorrect reading at a critical moment.

There has been a great deal of research on human error and catastrophic accidents in several safety-critical industries besides maritime (eg nuclear, air, road, rail, defence). A universal finding is that it is combinations of multiple adverse circumstances that create disastrous outcomes. It is not human mistake-making that is the problem, so much as the existing conditions and history of the organisation in which it occurs.

Consider, for example, the tragic case of the passenger ferry *MS Scandinavian Star*.

### Case study: Fatal fire on *MS Scandinavian Star*[2]

Early in 1990, Scandinavian World Cruises sold *MS Scandinavian Star*, a casino ship, to Vognmandsruten for use as a passenger ferry between Oslo, Norway and Frederikshavn,

---

[2] Based on Wikipedia (2009) with further interpretation by the authors

Denmark. While *en route* on 7 April, 1990 an arsonist set a fire (probably two fires) on Deck 3 in the passenger section. The brand new crew were mostly Filipino and had no Norwegian or English. Due to the ship's schedule, they had undergone training for the ship's new ferry duties in only 10 days, a good month short of the time they might have expected for orientation and work-up for such a ship.

Now, it was the middle of the night and, helped by the ventilation fans in the car storage area, the fire quickly spread throughout Deck 3 and onwards to Decks 4 and 5. The fire was also assisted by the highly flammable melamine resin laminate that covered many of the surfaces. As it burned, the resin gave off two extremely poisonous gases (hydrogen cyanide and carbon monoxide) which would asphyxiate most of the 158 people who died as the tragedy unfolded.

As the fire spread, the Captain ordered the fire doors on Deck 3 to be closed. But they could not be operated remotely – and some had been wedged open. The fire was too far advanced. Reasoning that the fire was being fed by the air conditioning system, the Captain ordered the system to be turned off. However, the result was that toxic smoke now entered the passenger cabins and began to suffocate people who were already trapped by the fire and smoke in the passageways.

Alarms were sounded, distress signals were broadcast and the order was given to abandon ship. But the alarms were largely unheard and many people did not wake up before they were fatally overcome by toxic smoke. Others could not find their way to the exits. Unfamiliar with the ship or how to deal with the fire, and unable to communicate with passengers anyway, the largely untrained crew could do little except abandon ship. Unaware of the evacuation progress, the Captain and crew later discovered that many passengers had been left aboard. One third of the passengers died. One was a woman who was six months pregnant.

Sixteen years later, in 2006, a memorial was erected near the Akershus Fortress in Oslo. Along with a plaque inscribed with the names of all the victims, it depicts a mother and her child.

It is, of course, indisputable that this disaster would not have happened if there had been no arson. It is also clear that the Captain's assumptions about the role of the Deck 3 exhaust fans and ship's air conditioning system were mistaken – or at least incomplete. But it should also be clear that the catalogue of mistakes for this event must include several serious organisational errors, including:

- The design decision to use melamine resin laminate 20 years before, when the ship was built

- The design decision to require manual fire door operation

- The design specification for alarm systems that proved to be inadequate when they were needed

- The design solution for escape routes in the presence of smoke and fire

- The management decision to hire crew who could not communicate with passengers

- The management decision to deploy crew unfamiliar with the ship and inadequately trained for responding to fire

> A mistake is what hindsight sees. Until then, it is an action just like any other.

Given the operational and economic pressures to start the ship on its new ferry route, these decisions are clearly the result of trade-offs between efficiency and thoroughness at an organisational level (see section on *Making decisions*). Note, too, that while some of these trade-offs were made in the days and weeks before the disaster, others were made *decades* before.

The important thing to understand is that disasters like the one that befell the *Scandinavian Star* are never attributable to a single error and nor are they only attributable to the people 'at the sharp end' – ie the Captain and crew. The organisational culture, operational pressures and prevailing management style all provide a powerful context for the behaviour of the workforce.

As made clear in the sections on *Making decisions* and *Taking risks*, people's behaviour – at all organisational levels – is more like a deft, smooth flow around the obstacles they encounter. This flow makes perfect sense at the time to all involved. It is only later, when things have gone wrong that some of their decisions and actions are re-interpreted as mistakes.

### How can we stop mistakes from becoming disasters?

There are two distinct approaches to this question. One is traditional and assumes that the things that happen are in principle predictable and are due to cause and effect. The other has become much more important recently and assumes that many of the things that happen emerge unpredictably from the behaviour of complex systems.

### Things happen due to cause and effect…don't they?

This is still the dominant way of thinking about mistakes and accidents in our modern world. It is based on the apparent obviousness of cause and effect. It is possible to look at the mistakes listed for the *Scandinavian Star* disaster and interpret them as a complicated series of causes and effects that interacted over time to inevitably result in the catastrophe that happened.

In this view, when disaster happens (or when we can imagine it happening), it seems correct to root out and fix (or pre-empt) the causes that might have bad effects. So, accident investigators use *root cause analysis* techniques to discover primary and secondary causes. Meanwhile, organisational safety specialists perform risk assessments to try and avert any dangerous effects of work procedures. The results of accident investigations

and corporate due diligence are typically enshrined in rule books and methodology statements that grow bigger every year. The logic of this approach is to get to a point where all the possible sources of error have been eliminated or covered by a rule or procedure that will prevent them from occurring. There are four problems with this approach.

> "Knowledge and error flow from the same mental sources: only success can tell one from the other"
>
> Ernst Mach, physicist and philosopher (1905)

- **Efficiency usually wins**. Where rules and procedures collide with the need to be efficient due to economic considerations, we find ways to work around them. The more thorough the rules and procedures are, the more efficiencies will be found (see section on *Making decisions*), subject to the risks perceived (see section on *Taking risks*).

- **Behaviour drifts towards danger**. If the efficiencies that we use to meet our schedules and targets do not result in an accident over a long time, the organisation may drift – often unnoticed – towards and across safety limits. This is sometimes referred to as complacency. However, labelling it as such and issuing warnings about it is highly unlikely to challenge those of us who, as far as we are concerned, are operating within acceptable levels of risk (see section on *Taking risks*).

- **Mistakes are invisible when they are made**. An error is usually only noticed or labelled as such when it has already contributed to catastrophe. Before that, it is simply one of many actions or decisions made as part of the smooth, efficient flow of workplace activity.

- **Accidents keep happening anyway**. However explicable accidents are seen to be in terms of causes and effects after they happen, the fact is, nobody saw them as such at the time. Furthermore, despite all we have learned from cause and effect analysis, huge and costly maritime disasters are still occurring at the rate of nearly one a week, not to mention the thousands of accidents in which seafarers lose their fingers, limbs and livelihoods and their employers lose their expertise, reputations and viability.

In fact, each of these four problems are aspects of hindsight – the illusion that the world is completely predictable. Mach's quote on this page illustrates the true position of hindsight. It is a useful tool for historical investigators, but of no value whatsoever to anyone who is at the point of a decision. This is because when we are required to decide or act, we do not yet know the significance of our decision. Only history will tell us – or others – if our decision will be interpreted as a mistake. At the moment of our decision we can only be guided by the sense we can make of our situation (based on our training, experience, and immersion in our

> Hindsight is the illusion that the world is completely predictable.

Recent developments in our increasingly globalised world – such as the world of shipping – emphasise the need to see it more as a complex system of interacting, circular relationships rather than a linear sequence of causes and effects. What developments have produced this changed view?

- **Rapid technological change** Technology is changing too fast for managers and engineers to keep up. This is affecting all parts of the maritime industry, eg bridge automation and navigation systems, real-time global tracking and management of vessels by their land-based owners, and high-tech vessel design and operation (eg LNG tankers).

- **New ways to fail** Digital technologies create new kinds of failure and new kinds of accident. The traditional safety engineering approach of using redundancy to minimise risks does not work with (eg) computer systems where redundancy adds complexity and thereby actually increases risk.

- **Bigger disasters** The scale and expense of modern systems means that the human and financial harm resulting from accidents is becoming less acceptable. Learning from experience is not tolerable, and the emphasis must be on preventing even a single accident.

- **More complexity** The development of highly complex systems frequently means that no one person understands the whole system or has complete control of it. Furthermore, the circumstances of their use can never be completely specified and the resulting variability of performance is unavoidable.

- **More serious knock-on effects** Systems are increasingly tightly linked. This means a disturbance in one part of the system can have rapid, far-ranging and unpredictable ripple effects. It also means that many adverse events cannot be attributed to breakdown of components, but may be the result of unexpected combinations of performance variability that is essentially normal. In this view, adverse events are simply the other side of the coin from equally unexpected but beneficial events.

organisational culture – see section on *Making sense of things*) and the risks we are willing to take (see section on *Taking risks*).

Cause and effect analysis makes sense of history with the benefit of hindsight. It allows feedback to be gathered about the effectiveness (or not) of people's actions and to learn from those that can be re-classified as mistakes. However, when it comes to helping people in the live, real-time environment of the workplace, it is less than adequate, and may actually be a hindrance.

This is because a rule created to prevent the repeat of a past mistake is rooted in the circumstances that generated that mistake. If those circumstances are rare or do not occur again, the rule may be seen simply as an additional piece of bureaucracy that must be worked round in the interests of efficiency.

### Things happen due to complex system behaviour

If the world is not completely predictable as a series of causes and effects, how can it be understood sufficiently well to stop serious mistakes in their tracks?

Doing so requires a shift of view – driven by a number of observations about the way in which the world has changed in recent years (see panel, *How is the world different now?*).

This shift of view emphasises the world as a complex system of interacting, circular relationships. This is also



Traditionally, increasing safety rules and procedures seems a reasonable way to increase safety. After all, if safety is enshrined in a framework of rules that is erected around us, this provides a means of recognising unsafe behaviour and enables consistent training to measurable standards.

But the framework also locates safety outside people, shaping their behaviour, constraining it to flow one way rather than another. When reality inevitably pokes through and injures someone, the usual response is to plug the hole with another rule. The ever more detailed lattice creates an ever greater training (and regulation) task, and increases the rigidity of the behaviour it constrains.

By contrast, Morel's recent study of fishing skippers confirmed earlier French Air Force findings about pilots that safety is self-managed. Safety is a component of decision making (and risk taking) that resides inside people as part of their expertise. The study showed that skilled people with clear goals in high-risk situations constantly present themselves (and their colleagues) with new challenges. Their decisions to do so are based on their sense of their own ability to anticipate the real risks, and their confidence in managing surprises. Indeed, part of their decision making is driven by the need to further refine and calibrate their judgment by exposing themselves to risk.

Observers of fishing skippers and fighter pilots would readily agree that their behaviour is not overly constrained by prescriptive safety rules. If it was, they could not function. Morel's analysis underlines safety as an emergent property of a person's task performance as they engage with their environment. Over time, their developing expertise becomes better tuned to the real risks of the job.

Of course it is the case that some external safety guidance must be available. If there were none, people would have to repeatedly and independently invent their own safety goals and standards, leading to inconsistency and avoidable accidents. Potential for an effective compromise between the two positions of constraint-based safety and self-managed safety lies in the concept of goal-based rules. Here, principles and standards are set, but the means for achieving them is left to the natural human strength of adaptable expertise operating, as it must, in dynamic and uncertain environments.

*Sources: Morel (2008) and Earthy & Sherwood Jones (2006)*

known as systems thinking. It is out of these interactions that behaviour – both good and bad – emerges. This systems view brings into focus a number of important points relating to humans and the organisations they create. Here are three.

### Humans create safety

In the systems view, people are not seen as sources of error so much as the creators of safety (see panel on previous page, *Where is safety – in people or in rules?*). This view recognises that there will always be gaps in any system because designers and rule makers cannot envisage all situations and contingencies. This means that human operators must be given some degree of freedom to cope with the unexpected. In turn, this increases the need for the human operator to identify and manage the risks that arise.

### Organisations are actually organic

In the systems view, organisations are not static, and safety emerges continuously from the overall behaviour of an organisation's interacting components – including its people. Many forces, such as political or economic concerns, can cause an organisation to drift away from safety. A good safety record can promote complacency, allowing risks to grow unseen. Perhaps the most common threat to safety is when change in one part of an organisation's functioning unwittingly disturbs functioning in some other part of the organisation.

### Organisations create the behaviour they get

In the systems view, organisations are seen as operating within a commercial framework including shareholders, unions, financial institutions, competitors, suppliers, and so on. They also operate within a legal, regulatory and political framework – several such frameworks if they operate in multiple countries. Other influences include the range of social and demographic factors that contribute to the educational levels of new recruits, and the difficulties of recruiting, motivating and retaining staff. There is also the behaviour of the public, and the incidence of crime, terrorism, vandalism and piracy and much else besides. Last, but not least, the technology provided by an organisation also produces its own influences on the role, ability and expectations of its users, as well as the entire organisational culture.

Organisations create the behaviour they get and they get the behaviour they deserve. This is because any given organisation (system) is capable of generating a range of outputs, all of which emerge from the interaction of its parts. In a healthy organisation, most of these outputs will be relevant and beneficial to the organisation. Sometimes, the emergent behaviour may seem surprisingly beneficial, eg when someone discovers a new and highly efficient way to accomplish an important objective. Sometimes, however, at the other extreme, the behaviour that emerges will turn out to be adverse, eg when an accident happens. In every case, the behaviour that emerges from an organisation is always within the range of its own natural variability. Both highly beneficial and highly adverse behaviour should be expected: they are two sides of the same coin.

> "Managing organisational risks with safety statistics is like driving a car by watching the white line in the rear view mirror "
>
> Myron Tribus, TQM guru

### *Protecting organisations from things that happen*

Rules and procedures are designed to limit system variability. If they are followed, they may help to avert accidents up to a point, but they also prevent beneficially novel behaviour from emerging too. As maritime organisations, their people and their technologies become more complex and more tightly bound together with each other, the potential for unpredictable adverse behaviour with devastating knock-on effects also increases.

At the same time, the increasing number of rules demanded by the traditional cause-and-effect view not only becomes less and less effective, but also becomes counter-productive as people search for more efficient ways through the bureaucracy. So if more rules and procedures aren't always the answer, what else can organisations do to avert disasters such as the *Scandinavian Star*?

Recent research into the resilience of some safety-critical organisations has revealed some of the reasons why the more successful ones have far fewer accidents than they should.

Here are three reasons with particular relevance for the maritime industry:

- **Expertise must be developed, retained and exploited.** In the face of pressure for greater efficiencies, people at all organisational levels work hard to understand the routes to failure and to develop alternative strategies, while all the time creating and maintaining whatever safety margins they can. Central to their success is the depth of their expertise. It permits them to read complex situations, project into the future, and to follow timely and effective courses of action (see section on *Making decisions*). Organisations that fail to invest in developing such expertise, or that fail to protect their experts from the legal and corporate consequences that flow from the decisions they took in good faith, will ultimately fail economically. The experts will leave as soon as they perceive the risk to them is too great. For example, one reason why it has become increasingly common for Masters to get shore jobs as soon as they are qualified is to avoid potentially serious criminal charges should they make a mistake.

- **Organisations must pay attention to their 'fault lines'.** Assessment of the risks of operational error or adverse events often miss the point that the real risk to safety-critical operations is in the interfaces – the natural fault lines – between an organisation's different parts. These include the 'fault lines' between training and practice; managers and operators; designers and users; shipowners and crews; officers and ratings; efficiency and thoroughness. Focusing on the real risks is one challenge. Another is knowing how these risks are changing over time and, in particular, how far the organisation is drifting towards dangerous levels of behaviour. Many maritime organisations collect data on accidents and near misses. However, most then analyse this data for 'missing' rules rather than to optimise interfaces or detect and correct dangerous drift.

- **Decision making must be based on systems thinking.** All safety-critical industries are formed of different organisations which must interface successfully. In the maritime industry, these include shipbuilders, shipowners and managers, Masters and crews, port authorities, flags, insurance clubs and so on. In the absence of applied systems thinking, organisational decisions are taken that are locally optimised (ie too narrowly-focused on a small part of the problem) at the expense of global effectiveness. There are countless examples of this in the maritime industry – mostly driven by apparent opportunities to save money in the immediate future.

> ## You have to use systems thinking. Finance Directors – this means YOU!

## So who is accountable – and what can be done?

It is clear that it is normal for us to make mistakes. It is also clear that wider organisational factors play a huge part in helping to create our behaviour – including our mistakes. These twin realisations have allowed a new approach to safety management to emerge in recent years. The key insight has hinged on the need for safety-critical organisations to shift from a blame culture to a 'just culture'.

A 'just culture' is founded on two principles[3], which apply simultaneously to *everyone* in the organisation:

- Human error is inevitable and the organisations' policies, processes and interfaces must be continually monitored and improved to accommodate those errors.

- Individuals should be accountable for their actions if they knowingly violate safety procedures or policies.

Achieving both of these two principles is enormously challenging. The first principle requires a reporting system and culture that people can trust enough to make the necessary disclosures. Their trust develops out of the way the second principle is implemented – specifically from the way in which the organisation defines, investigates and attributes accountability for whatever its staff disclose.

---

[3] GAIN Working Group E (2004)

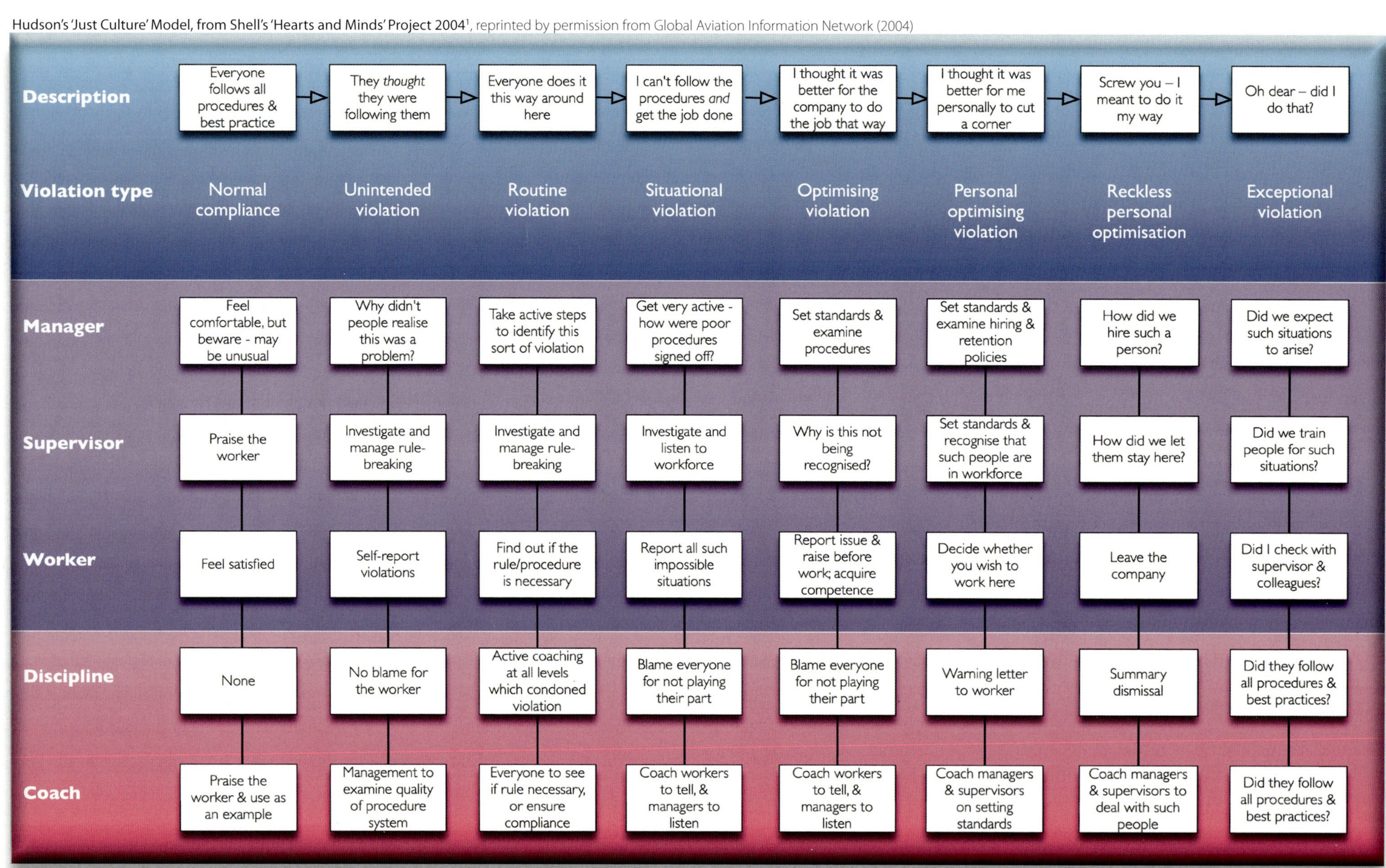

| | Normal compliance | Unintended violation | Routine violation | Situational violation | Optimising violation | Personal optimising violation | Reckless personal optimisation | Exceptional violation |
|---|---|---|---|---|---|---|---|---|
| **Description** | Everyone follows all procedures & best practice | They *thought* they were following them | Everyone does it this way around here | I can't follow the procedures *and* get the job done | I thought it was better for the company to do the job that way | I thought it was better for me personally to cut a corner | Screw you – I meant to do it my way | Oh dear – did I do that? |
| **Violation type** | Normal compliance | Unintended violation | Routine violation | Situational violation | Optimising violation | Personal optimising violation | Reckless personal optimisation | Exceptional violation |
| **Manager** | Feel comfortable, but beware - may be unusual | Why didn't people realise this was a problem? | Take active steps to identify this sort of violation | Get very active - how were poor procedures signed off? | Set standards & examine procedures | Set standards & examine hiring & retention policies | How did we hire such a person? | Did we expect such situations to arise? |
| **Supervisor** | Praise the worker | Investigate and manage rule-breaking | Investigate and manage rule-breaking | Investigate and listen to workforce | Why is this not being recognised? | Set standards & recognise that such people are in workforce | How did we let them stay here? | Did we train people for such situations? |
| **Worker** | Feel satisfied | Self-report violations | Find out if the rule/procedure is necessary | Report all such impossible situations | Report issue & raise before work; acquire competence | Decide whether you wish to work here | Leave the company | Did I check with supervisor & colleagues? |
| **Discipline** | None | No blame for the worker | Active coaching at all levels which condoned violation | Blame everyone for not playing their part | Blame everyone for not playing their part | Warning letter to worker | Summary dismissal | Did they follow all procedures & best practices? |
| **Coach** | Praise the worker & use as an example | Management to examine quality of procedure system | Everyone to see if rule necessary, or ensure compliance | Coach workers to tell, & managers to listen | Coach workers to tell, & managers to listen | Coach managers & supervisors on setting standards | Coach managers & supervisors to deal with such people | Did they follow all procedures & best practices? |

## How should accountability be assessed?

### Honest mistake – or negligence?

For the purposes of assessing accountability, many professions try to discriminate between mistakes which are 'honest' (eg due to lack of training or experience) or 'negligent' (eg due to lack of diligence or attention). Unfortunately, there is a problem with 'negligence' since, as we have seen, there are many organisational reasons for an experienced person's deliberate rule-breaking or distraction at a critical moment. In the end, the line between the two turns on who draws it – and for what reason.

### Legal accountability: fairy tales with unhappy endings

A major problem in examining an incident in terms of its historical chain of presumed causes and effects is that the story often suffers from the powerful effects of hindsight bias. This bias results in the following:

- Causality is oversimplified
- The 'obviousness' of the outcome is overestimated
- The role of rule violations is overestimated
- The relevance of information used (or not used) by people before the incident is overestimated

When a legal approach is used to investigate 'negligence' cases, the outcome is almost never 'just', and safety usually suffers. The prosecution tends to fashion selected evidence into a simply understood story that is focused on the defendant, who ends up as an organisational scapegoat. This outcome produces fear and mistrust, discourages further safety reporting and drives unsafe behaviour underground. Criminalising honestly made professional error is entirely counter-productive.

### Organic accountability: 'just' desserts

Accountability in a 'just culture' is assessed by investigating how actions and decisions made sense to each involved person at all levels of the organisation at the time of the incident, and what changes the organisation could consider to prevent them from contributing to a mistake again.

Reporting is supported by debriefing programmes to help cope with trauma. Investigations are conducted by expert practitioners who have deep knowledge of the technical demands of the incident and are schooled in hindsight bias. Techniques such as 'substitution' may be used in which experts can mentally place themselves in the incident to decide what they would have reasonably done.

The different perspectives may then be assembled into a 'mosaic' to form a rich picture of the incident. Note, however, that no-one had this picture at the time of the incident, and it is only useful to help consider what systemic changes might be necessary.

One of the most comprehensive attempts to combine the major elements of a 'just culture' is the 'Hearts and Minds' project launched company-wide by Shell in 2004. Hudson's model (opposite) is based on earlier work[4] and describes the different types of violation, accountability and follow-up disciplinary and learning actions at all organisational levels.

> **Accountability is best accomplished within a 'just culture'**

### What are the aims and benefits of a 'just culture'?

Besides Shell, 'just culture' programmes have been initiated in other safety-critical organisations, including BP Shipping, Teekay Marine Services, a number of aviation authorities and the health sector. These programmes usually describe a journey or ladder, together with supporting tools designed to change the safety attitudes of the entire workforce.

The journey is typically depicted as moving through a number of organisational approaches to safety. This may start with the 'pathological' stage, where people don't really care about safety at all and expect someone to get fired if there is an accident. At the end of the journey is the 'generative' stage where people actively seek information, and failures lead to far reaching reforms (see panel on next page, *The safety culture ladder*).

The following benefits of a 'just culture' are anticipated[5]:

[4] Reason (1997)
[5] GAIN Working Group E (2004)

The safety culture ladder is a safety maturity model that was adopted by the oil and gas industry following an OGP (Oil and Gas Producers) meeting in the Hague in 2000. It is now being used within BP Shipping, Teekay Marine Services and Shell's Hearts and Minds project. Here are its five stages and their characteristics, starting from the top (most mature).

**Level 5: Generative**
- Managers know what's happening – the workforce tells them
- Bad news is sought out so failures can be learned from
- People are constantly aware of what could go wrong
- Safety is seen as a profit centre

**Level 4: Proactive**
- Resources are allocated to anticipate and prevent incidents
- Management is open to bad news, but still focused on statistics
- The workforce is trusted and feels involved in safety

**Level 3: Calculative**
- There are lots of audits and lots of data to describe things
- The new Safety Management System is assumed to be enough
- People are surprised when incidents still happen
- Bad news is tolerated

**Level 2: Reactive**
- Safety is taken seriously every time there is an accident
- Managers try to force compliance with rules and procedures
- Many discussions are held to re-classify incidents
- Bad news is kept hidden

**Level 1: Pathological**
- We leave it to the lawyers or regulators to decide what's OK
- There are bound to be accidents – this is a dangerous business
- If someone is stupid enough to have an accident, sack them
- Bad news is unwelcome – kill the messenger

*Source: http://info.ogp.org.uk/HF/ (in Mar '10) following work by Hudson & Parker (2002), reproduced with permission*

- Increased reporting of unsafe incidents and accidents – including trends that indicate future problems developing

- Increased trust between all levels of the workforce – which accelerates the organisation's journey towards greater safety maturity

- Decreased actual numbers of adverse incidents and accidents

- Decreased operational costs – due to safer behaviour, higher workforce motivation and morale, and increased productivity

This last benefit has allowed Shell to make a convincing case for safety within a 'just culture' to be transformed from a cost centre to a profit centre.

## What are the problems in developing a 'just culture'?

The journey to a 'just culture' involves some difficult challenges. Research carried out in several safety-critical industries shows that a central task is designing an incident-reporting system and integrating it with a process for assessing individual accountability across the whole organisation. The new reporting system may be quite different from any existing incident reporting system. Some of the main requirements for this task are set out in the panel, *Steps towards a 'just culture'*.

Another key task is the design of a series of easy-to-use diagnostic and reflective tools. These help the workforce – at all organisational levels – understand where they



**Address corporate and legal issues**
- Need to obtain unambiguous boardroom commitment
- Need to create indemnity for incident reporters against legal proceedings – this may require changes to existing legislation
- Need to separate reporting system staff from disciplinary staff

**Design and integrate reporting system**
- Need to identify responsibilities and incident report investigators with domain expertise in safety, operations, management and HR
- Need to create a rapid, efficient reporting process that captures and yields useful information at the right level of detail
- Need to create clear, easily-accessible process that will be used and trusted
- Need to decide if new process will be integrated with current incident-reporting procedure
- Need to create investigative and assessment processes for deciding accountabilities and action

**Develop, promote and roll out reporting system**
- Need to identify and assign development resources
- Need to identify champion(s) and communications strategy
- Need to educate users
- Need to collect feedback from users
- Need to feed back useful results to users at all organisational levels – including impact on production, efficiency, communication and cost benefits

*Derived from a document for which permission to reprint was given by the Global Aviation Information Network – GAIN Working Group E (2004)*

are in the journey, together with the nature of the gaps between their current attitudes and behaviours and those they need to acquire. Tools are also needed to support the acquisition of the required behaviours. One of the most advanced toolsets has been developed as part of Shell's 'Hearts and Minds' programme. This toolset has now been made publicly available following a publishing agreement between the Energy Institute and Shell. It includes short (five-minute to half-day) structured sessions aimed at improving the following:

- Driving and driver manager behaviour

- Safe working

- Supervisory behaviour

- Rule-breaking

- Situation awareness

- Understanding and assessing personal risk

- Making change last

- Seeing yourself as others see you

- Understanding own organisational culture

Notably, many of the items addressed in the Hearts and Minds toolset are also key topics within this Guide. It is no accident that the same qualities that make us human are also the main focus of enlightened organisations' recognition that their employees need to work together equitably within a culture that is judged to be 'just' by all.

## DO's

DO recognise that mistake making is part of normal human behaviour. The variability of human behaviour is generated in part by the organisational systems that we participate in, and it acquires meaning from the backcloth of organisational culture that we contribute to, and are influenced by.

DO look for the downside of any cost-oriented changes in your organisation: cost reduction will always drive people to greater efficiency at the expense of thoroughness, leading to more mistakes and less capacity or inclination to catch them.

DO whatever you can to help design and implement a 'just culture' in your organisation. It needs to be based on the transparent accountability of individuals at all levels of the organisation and open and honest incident reporting. It will not only improve safety, but transform safety into a profit centre.

## DONT's

DON'T be misled by the apparent power of hindsight: it is useful to historians and accident investigators, but never to anyone who needs to act in the moment. Hindsight is an artificial position that lies outside the stream of operational activity. It enables actions to be re-labelled as mistakes, and action sequences to be re-told as if they were inevitable stories. It allows insight after the event, but it is never available to the characters in the story.

DON'T imagine that one day there can be a rule for every eventuality. Behaviour emerges from complex interactions between people and the systems of which they are part. It is not completely predictable in principle.

## Around the buoys again

The main points covered by this section are as follows.

It is normal for people to make mistakes. These may be skill-based, rule-based or knowledge-based.

Mistakes are made more likely by 'people' factors such as fatigue, stress, training, experience and communications; and organisational factors such as time, equipment design, staffing, and safety culture.

Organisational culture, pressures and prevailing management style provide a powerful context for people's behaviour.

The traditional view of accidents as cause-effect chains is only possible with hindsight. Before an adverse incident, decisions and actions are all part of a deft, smooth flow of activity 'in the moment' in which all parties are doing the best they can with available resources.

Hindsight is the illusion that the world is predictable in principle. Analysis of accidents in terms of causes and effects is useful for identifying changes to existing procedures. However, the goal of eliminating all sources of error is futile. This is because there is good evidence that adverse events are simply part of the range of behaviour that emerges from the interactions of all of the component system parts. In this view, organisations create the behaviour they get, and they get the behaviour they deserve.

Progress towards a safety culture that fully accommodates the organisational influences on human behaviour – including mistake-making – can be made by the pursuit of a 'just culture'. This allows the accountabilities of individuals at all levels of the organisation to be properly addressed and fairly integrated.

The journey to a fully mature 'just culture' presents difficult challenges, but promises to create much more effective safety based on genuine attitude change. It also provides the means to transform safety from a cost centre into a profit centre.

## Deeper waters

This section has drawn on the following materials:

Bailey N. (2007) *Marine Incidents: Ways of Seeing, SIRC Symposium 2007*, Seafarers International Research Centre, Cardiff University

Dekker S.W.A. (2007) *Just Culture: Balancing safety and Accountability*, Ashgate Publishing Ltd

Earthy J.V. & Sherwood Jones B.M. (2006) *Design for the human factor: the move to goal-based rules*, Lloyds Register

Energy Institute (2009) *Hearts and Minds Programme*, http://www.eimicrosites.org/heartsandminds/index.php (in Mar, 10)
GAIN Working Group E (2004) *A Roadmap to a Just Culture: Enhancing the Safety Environment*, First Edition, Sep 2004, Flight Ops/ATC Ops Safety Information Sharing

Hollnagel E. (2009) *The ETTO Principle: Efficiency - Thoroughness Trade-Off: Why Things That Go Right Sometimes Go Wrong*, Ashgate Publishing Ltd

Hudson P. (2007) *What is the Hearts and Minds Programme?* Powerpoint presentation at http://www.riskinsite.com.au/sicorp_web/Events/07OHSSeminar/Day%201/Patrick%20Hudson.ppt (in Sep 09)

Morel G., Amalberti R. & Chuavin C. (2008) *Articulating the differences between safety and resilience: the decision making process of professional sea-fishing skippers*, Human Factors Vol 50, No. 1, February 2008 pp 1-16

Rasmussen J. (1979): *On the Structure of Knowledge – a Morphology of Mental Models in a Man-Machine System Context*. Risø-M-2192, 1979

Reason J. (1990) *Human Error*. New York: Cambridge University Press

Reason J. (1997) *Managing the risks of organisational accidents*, Hants, England, Ashgate Publishing Ltd

Shell (2006) *The Shell Sustainability Report 2006*, http://sustainabilityreport.shell.com/2006/responsibleenergy/personalandprocesssafety/changingbehaviour.html (in Mar '10)

Wikipedia (2009) *MS Scandinavian Star*, http://en.wikipedia.org/wiki/MS_Scandinavian_Star (in Mar '10)

# Getting tired and stressed

## How much of a problem is fatigue?

Before 1989, it had been common knowledge for thousands of years that seafaring and fatigue went hand in hand. Then, on a cold midnight in March, the single hulled *Exxon Valdez* struck Bligh Reef off Alaska. The tanker spilt 11 million US gallons of crude oil into the sea. The slick eventually covered 11 million square miles of ocean (a gallon of crude goes a long way), creating the most devastating man-made environmental sea disaster in history. Hundreds of thousands of sea creatures died. Within two years, the local marine population and fishing industry had all but collapsed. Several residents, including a former mayor, committed suicide and the Alaska Native Corporation went bankrupt. Billions of dollars were paid in damages and fines. The shoreline will not recover until 2020.

At the time of the accident, there were two crew members on the bridge. The Third Mate, then aged 25, was in charge of the wheel house and an Able Seaman was at the helm. Neither had been given their mandatory six hours off duty before their 12-hour duty began. Amongst its main findings, the US National Transportation Safety Bureau's (NTSB) accident investigators concluded that the Exxon Shipping Company's manning policies *"did not adequately consider the increase in workload caused by reduced manning"*.

The widely-shared belief that fatigue played a significant part in marine incidents had been made official. Yet, despite that unambiguous finding 20 years ago, the issues of reduced manning, increased workload and resulting fatigue have continued to play a major role in many maritime accidents to the present day.

Reduced manning is an organisational policy aimed at increasing efficiency. It is often made possible by the introduction of automation. As we show elsewhere in this Guide (see section on *Making decisions*), increased efficiency usually means a corresponding decrease in thoroughness[1]. Automation solves some problems at the expense of creating others. In the case of the unfortunate crew on *Exxon Valdez*, the demands placed on them increased fatigue to the point where it became a serious threat to safety.

## What causes fatigue?

Rather obviously, people get tired when they have been awake too long. But how long is "too long"? Several factors affect this, as follows:

- **Workload** The harder people work, the sooner they need time to recover from it. Workload itself is influenced by the design of the tools, equipment and procedures people must use, and the expertise they have acquired through training and experience. In fact, the problem of workload and its measurement is a little more complicated than it looks at first sight. This is because it is the result of a mix of external and subjective factors – see panel, *Why is workload a tricky problem?*



---

### Why is workload a tricky problem?

**It's hard to define**
There is little agreement on what workload actually is. Some researchers focus on the external demands of a working situation. Others concentrate on the person's experience of workload.

**It's hard to measure**
As a result, it is very difficult to answer the question 'How much workload is safe?' Additionally, no clear relationships have been found between measures of external demand, subjective assessment and physiological indications of workload.

**It's fickle**
Workload fluctuates over a work period. There are peak periods when a person cannot attend to all the demands placed on them. But workload is also an issue when the person is working hard over an extended period. Even though the workload may never reach peak demands, the cumulative effect may be a safety issue.

**It means different things**
The weight of demand a person can cope with is one focus for workload. But another focus is to do with the pattern of demands. For example, talking on a mobile phone while driving a car is not generally considered to be a weighty workload task, but all the evidence points to the greatly increased risk of an accident. Being distracted or having to switch tasks occupies more of our attention and memory, and increases the risk of making a mistake.

**It's two problems**
Workload problems usually refer to having too much to do. But having too little to do can equally put safety at risk. Boredom and monotony are as fatiguing as heavy workloads.

**Bottom line**
The bottom line is that a person's experience of workload is a combination of both the actual external demands of the job and the individual characteristics and expertise of the person doing the job. The challenge that remains is to find a workload assessment method that takes proper account of both of sides of the equation.

- **Sleep debt** People need enough sleep of the right sort to recover from their wakeful activities. In its absence, they build up a 'sleep debt' which severely affects their ability to stay alert. Sleep debt causes people to misread situations, overlook key information and fall asleep even when they know it will put them and their colleagues at extreme risk.

- **Perceived risk or interest** If people are stimulated by their sense of risk or interest in what they are doing, they can stay awake and alert for longer. However, the time they then need to recover from sustained activity will also get longer. If people are engaged on tedious or boring tasks, they will feel tired sooner. People often increase their exposure to risk in order to create the levels of interest and alertness they need (see section on *Taking risks*).

- **Diet** Inadequate levels of nutrition accelerate the onset of fatigue. Different foods also affect alertness. For example, heavier meals dominated by carbohydrates encourage sleepiness, while lighter, protein-based meals encourage wakeful alertness.

- **Fitness and movement** People who are overweight and/ or lacking in exercise will tend to feel fatigued earlier than their leaner, fitter or more active colleagues.

- **Time of day** People live by natural daily rhythms, which means that they feel least alert in the small hours of the morning and most alert in the period before midday.

- **Environment** People become more fatigued in environments with bad levels of light, noise, vibration, temperature and motion. Research has shown that some aromas, such as lemon scent, encourage alertness.

Of these factors, the crew of the *Exxon Valdez* were certainly suffering from the effects of workload and sleep debt. The contribution of the other factors is not known. A lot was learned about the role of fatigue in maritime accidents as a result of this incident. However, the knowledge gained has done little to eliminate the problem. Let's have a look at a much more recent incident – the *Antari* grounding – which took place nearly 20 years after the *Exxon Valdez*.

## Case study: Out for the count[2]

At midnight in late June 2008, the Chief Officer began his six-hour watch on the bridge of the general cargo vessel *Antari*. Seven hours before, she had left her berth at Corpach, Scotland after being loaded with 2,000 tonnes of scrap metal, bound for Ghent, Belgium. Now, as *Antari* headed south at 11 knots with the west coast of the Kintyre peninsula to her port side, the Chief Officer knew that the next course change would be in 11 miles, just off the Mull of Kintyre lighthouse. The new course would take them to the south east and on into the Irish Sea, so avoiding the Northern Irish coast over to their starboard. Earlier in the evening, the Chief Officer had excused the AB Lookout his 12-4 watch bridge duties due to the cargo duties and fabric maintenance the AB had carried out all day in Corpach. The Master had gone below for a well-earned rest immediately after handover and the Chief Officer was now the sole person on the bridge.

Both wheelhouse doors were closed; it was a clear, moonless night and the sea was calm with a slight westerly swell. As usual on *Antari*, the watch alarm had been deactivated so that the repeater units in the officer accommodation wouldn't wake the off-duty crew. The Chief Officer sat down, as was his custom, in a chair on the starboard side of the wheelhouse in front of one of the radar sets and the electronic chart display and information system (ECDIS) unit. And there, almost

Antari

immediately after sitting down, he fell asleep. He remained asleep until the vessel grounded on the Northern Ireland coast over three hours later. According to the UK's Marine Accident Investigation Branch (MAIB), 82% of the groundings that take place between 00.00 and 06.00 are due to fatigue, and *Antari* had just become one of them.

There were no injuries or pollution, and *Antari* was refloated with the tide three hours after she grounded. Following issue of an interim certificate in Belfast, and despite damage to 70% of her length, she was able to resume her voyage to Ghent. After discharging her cargo, she sailed on to Poland for repairs. It took several weeks and 25 tonnes of new steelwork before she was able to resume service.

When the Chief Officer had reported to the bridge that night, he was not showing any outward signs of fatigue (see panel, *What are the outward signs of fatigue?*). While the Chief Officer was responsible for cargo operations in port, the Master knew that little had been required of him the previous night between 19.00 and 09.00, and he had been able to rest in his cabin between 02.30 and 06.00.

So what had happened?

Subsequent investigation revealed the circumstances in which dangerous levels of fatigue had developed over time. *Antari* had made 21 port calls in the two months preceding the accident. Every port call had required the Master's and Chief Officer's intense involvement: preparations for arrival and departure, pilotage, supervision of cargo operations, official and cargo paperwork. Audits and statutory inspections were undertaken in port, and these additional demands could not all be met within the six hours on/six hours off watch pattern: they frequently required attention during what should have been rest periods.

This intensive pattern is typical of the short sea shipping trade and is known to contribute to the cumulative fatigue levels of people working six hours on/six hours off. *Antari* had just a seven-man crew, but this included a non-watchkeeping cadet. The Master and Chief Officer were the vessel's sole bridge watchkeeping officers, and they had worked six hours on/six hours off throughout the previous few months. They had both built up a significant 'sleep debt'. It was a time bomb waiting to go off. Furthermore, the bomb's fuse was shortened by the

> "Exhausted sentries will fall asleep, no matter what ... Savage punishment is no remedy ... There has to be some sleep".
>
> Lewis Keeble, MC, Canadian Company Commander
> Normandy Campaign, 1944



**Physical signs**

- Vacant stare with sunken, bloodshot eyes
- Eye strain, sore or 'heavy' eyes, dim or blurred vision
- Droning and humming in the ears
- Paleness of skin
- Slurred speech
- Headaches
- Feeling cold compared with others in the same room
- Faintness and dizziness
- Lack of energy, drowsiness
- Unstable posture/swaying, dropping chin, nodding head
- Loss of muscular strength, stiffness, cramps
- Loss of manual dexterity/difficulty making fine movements

**Operational signs**

- **Degraded mental performance** eg confusion, poor concentration, narrowed perception and forgetfulness. Leads to degraded vigilance and poor response to changing situations.

- **Diminished personal safety** Reduced self- and situation awareness leading to apathy, less attention to personal hygiene, neglect of normal safety precautions, and more risk taking.

- **Impaired leadership** Some people take longer to make decisions while others make poorer ones. The decision maker is often unaware of the decline. Fatigue can make people accept irrational, erroneous or illegal orders – or ignore good ones.

- **Worsening team performance** eg decreased interaction with crew members and degraded communication due to lower sensitivity to other people's needs and aims. People may lose their sense of humour and become moody, irritable, argumentative or socially withdrawn, all of which can badly affect crew relations.

- **Decreased morale** Fatigue decreases satisfaction, motivation and interest in team tasks and goals. Pessimism increases; people tend to think the worst, reject the group and take offence easily.

- **Odd behaviour** People may talk 'gibberish', neglect routine tasks, have stupid accidents and suffer hallucinations.

*Adapted from: Murphy (2002) with permission of Dir. of Psychology, Aus DoD*

unavailability of a bridge lookout, due to his own fatigue after a particularly demanding maintenance schedule: the Master liked to keep a very clean ship.

## What is 'sleep debt' and what causes it?

Humans live by a natural cycle of 24 hours, approximately 8 hours of which are required for sleeping. Unfortunately for safety-critical enterprises like seafaring, the human race evolved over millions of years to sleep at night.

These well-established natural rhythms mean that our bodies and brains are good for different things at different times of the 24-hour cycle. For example, a person's attention is worst between 02.00 and 06.00 and between 14.00 and 18.00 hours. It tends to be much better between 07.00 and 14.00 hours, and between 19.00 and 21.00.

At the end of an active session of wakefulness, we can become acutely fatigued. The performance of someone who has been awake for 24 hours is equivalent to that associated with a blood alcohol level 25% more than the current legal UK limit. This makes them seven times more likely to have an accident[3].

---

[3] Australian Government research (2000)



However, when we disrupt our natural rhythms on a regular basis, we need to do so extremely carefully, or we can become chronically fatigued. Those who must work shifts often sleep between one to four hours fewer than those in 'day jobs' in any 24-hour period. If sleep is missed, the need for sleep – 'sleep debt' – is built up.

> ## "24 hours without sleep has the same effect on performance as being 25% over the UK drink-drive limit"
> ### Australian Government (2000)

While sleep cannot be stored (eg by sleeping longer than a person needs to), a sleep debt must be repaid by seven to eight continuous hours of sleep in each 24-hour period over two or three days (see panel, *What happens when you sleep?*)

There are two main causes of sleep debt:

- **Disruptions to sleep itself** – such as loud noises, bright light, cold, heat, motion, sickness, chronic pain and infection.

- **Disruptions to natural sleep patterns**, such as shift work, operational demands (eg paperwork, ship inspections, drills and emergencies), personal worries, and inadequate, inappropriate or badly-timed food and fluids. One of the most distressing things for someone who is tired is to be given the opportunity to sleep, but to be unable to. Insomnia can be both a cause and an effect of increasing sleep debt, forming a vicious circle that must be broken before the effects of fatigue create serious consequences.

**Decreased attention and vigilance** People become less alert and slower to notice things. They may fail to detect signals or their significance, especially during monotonous tasks or in tedious environments. Tasks requiring sustained attention or surveillance are especially affected by fatigue.

**Communication difficulties** It becomes increasingly difficult to decide what needs to be said, how to say it, or what another said.

**Inability to concentrate** Maintaining focus on the task at hand, even for a few seconds, is difficult. People cannot follow complex directions or numerical calculations, and are easily confused.

**Omissions & carelessness** People increasingly skip steps, miss checks and make mistakes.

**Slower comprehension & learning** It takes increasingly longer to understand any written or spoken information, or display patterns, eg a map or charts.

**Slower information processing** It takes increasingly longer to transform data or process information, eg map coordinates are decoded slowly and mistakes are made doing it.

**Mood changes** Irritability, depression and apathy increases.

**Hallucinations** Extreme fatigue and low stimulation make people see, hear and act on things that appear very realistic, but illusory.

**Muddled thinking** Reasoning becomes slow and confused and deteriorates to irrational thoughts, poor logic and delusions.

**Faulty memory** Recall of recent events or orders becomes faulty. For example, the content of a radio message may be immediately forgotten or recalled incorrectly.

**Task complexity** Tasks that are complicated and boring are more seriously affected, compared with simpler, more interesting ones.

*Adapted from: Murphy (2002), with permission of Dir. of Psychology, Aus DoD*

## What are the effects of fatigue?

The main effects of fatigue on people at work are psychological. Of course, as the accident record shows, the mental effects on the individual can readily translate into catastrophic physical events, affecting individuals, businesses and the environment. The main effects of fatigue are summarised in the panel, *What are the effects of fatigue on performance?*

The most potentially damaging effects of fatigue are inattention, and the fact that fatigued people often fail to acknowledge that performance – both their own and others – is getting worse. These factors played major parts in both the *Exxon Valdez* and *Antari* incidents.

## How do you stop fatigue becoming a safety issue?

Fatigue is an ever-present fact of life. It happens to every one of us every single day. It must be dealt with via a mix of design and operational considerations.

### Design considerations

Fatigue can be reduced through good design. This means specifying ships, equipment, tools, procedures, manning levels, automation, training and regulation activities according to well-established principles of human factors and user-centred design[4]. Backed by an informed boardroom, design teams and procurement managers need to insist on a Human Factors Integration Plan for every new system or procedure (see panel, *What is a Human Factors Integration Plan?*).

[4] See MOD (2008) and US DoD (1999)



A Human Factors (HF) Integration Plan (HFIP) is a tool used by HF experts to ensure that all the key human issues are considered when an organisation is planning the procurement of a new system or work procedure. Below are the 12 HFIP elements used by London Underground Ltd.

1. **Responsibility** Who is in charge of HF for the project and what is their credential for doing so?

2. **Stakeholders** How will they be identified and consulted so that all the user requirements are specified as the project develops?

3. **Contractors and sub-contractors** How will they ensure sufficient attention to HF? (What and where is *their* HFIP?)

4. **Coordination** How are HF aspects to be coordinated across all parties involved? How will decisions be followed up?

5. **Management** How will HF considerations be incorporated into the regulatory consultation and approvals process?

6. **Operational concept** What is it, how does it fit with existing systems and procedures, and when will it be required?

7. **Legacy information** What can be re-used from existing systems to identify key aspects of users, processes, equipment, working conditions and safety?

8. **Design options assessment** How will the new system address user requirements, including capabilities, limitations, reliability, workload, health & safety, and hazard prevention?

9. **Standards** What HF standards and principles will be used during detailed design?

10. **Operability trials** What criteria will be used and how will performance be measured? What is the end user trials schedule? How will trials feedback be captured and used?

11. **Support** How will documentation, help facilities, and training development and delivery be implemented, and when?

12. **Evaluation** How will data on the performance of the system in use be collected, analysed and used?

*Adapted from LUL (2007), with permission*

With sympathetic support from the regulators and inspectors to ensure that such new systems and procedures are used, safe levels of alertness can be assured in the crews that must apply them.

As part of the Human Factors Integration Plan, the specific design activities relevant to avoiding undue fatigue relate to the following environmental factors[5]:

- **Lighting** Ship lighting systems are not powerful enough to overcome the natural human slow-down in the early morning that is associated with sleep. It has been found that installing special lighting systems that generate 1,000 times the light of normal systems helps people to adjust to night shift working by resetting the body's normal rhythm.

- **Noise** High levels of noise can impair hearing either permanently or temporarily and ship designers generally take account of this. However, continuous exposure to lower levels of background noise, eg from distant diesel engines, is a source of stress (see later in this section). Lower levels of continuous noise accelerate the onset of fatigue, disrupt restorative (deep) sleep and produce other tell-tale signs of stress such as high blood pressure and digestive problems. Noise levels of 40 to 50 dBA start to interfere with sleep. 70 dBA significantly disrupts sleep for almost everyone. Over and above the 'safe' limits, ship designers need to pay attention to the sources and pathways of noise and aim for quieter equipment, and better noise isolation, dampeners, barriers and absorption.

- **Vibration** Vibration from a ship's onboard machinery and ship movement affects everybody onboard. The crew are always in contact with one or another ship's surface, through which vibration is transmitted. Even quite brief exposure to vibration leads to fatigue and stress. Ship designers avoid levels of vibration known to lead directly to physiological damage. However, the recommended maritime limits of vibration guidelines are still high enough to significantly disrupt sleeping patterns, leading to the dangerous accumulation of sleep debt.

The bad effects of even 'safe' levels vibration are wide-ranging. Physiologically, they include changes to heart rate, breathing, blood flow and pressure. Seafarers can experience pain, nausea and problems with visual focusing, coordination and altered perceptions – all of which are sources of fatigue and stress. To reduce this problem, ship designers need to pay attention to increased dampening and isolation to reduce vibration to well below the current recommended levels.

- **Indoor climate** This includes temperature, ventilation and air quality. Safe limits for all these aspects are well known and already available to ship designers[6]. Like noise and vibration, however, the recommended levels tend to be focused on preventing harm, rather than fatigue. Getting too hot makes us feel tired and sleepy, reduces what we are able to do and leads us to make mistakes. Getting too cold lowers our levels of alertness and affects our ability to focus on what we are doing – particularly mental activities such as interpreting instruments or making calculations.

- **Ship motion** This is also a known source of fatigue and stress for seafarers. The problems of disrupted sleep through pitching and rolling are worsened by joint soreness caused by compensating movements of the lower back, knees and ankles during wakefulness.

It is clearly the business of ships to go to sea in all sorts of conditions, and to do so as profitably as possible. However, it is also the case that some design decisions have been informed by incomplete economic considerations that do not take account of everything that determines a shipowner's profits. For example, placing the deckhouse further aft on container ships both increases cargo capacity and allows faster, easier access to engineering spaces in the shipyard. But it also increases the exposure of the crew to the fatiguing effects of ship motion compared with that felt on lower decks, amidships and on the centre line.

The increase in the risk of ship loss produced by fatigued, sleep-indebted seafarers ought to be part of the economic calculation underlying such design decisions. Currently, it is largely overlooked.

**Fatigue kills. Careers. Clients. Crew.**

## Operational considerations

Operationally, people at all levels – from individual seafarers to boardroom directors – need to take fatigue, and particularly sleep debt, seriously. They need to avoid it or reduce it wherever they can. If they don't, it's only a matter of time before they or their organisation are involved in a potentially catastrophic incident.

Once a ship has been designed, commissioned and crewed, dangerous levels of fatigue and sleep debt can be averted in two ways:

- **Stick to the letter of the rules** Everyone needs to properly observe the existing rules and regulations about work/rest cycles. They are important and well-founded. Such mandates include EC Directive 1999/95/EC and STCW, as well as individual seafaring company and union regulations (see panel, *What do the work/rest rules say?*). These rules also make it a legal requirement for watch personnel to complete hours-of-rest records. However, it is suspected that only lip service is paid to this on a widespread basis, due to the pressure of operational demands (see next bullet). For example, on *Antari*, accident investigators found that watch personnel were pre-recording their hours irrespective of whether they were working or resting.

> ## The first key to fatigue is design – equipment, spaces and practices. The second is taking it seriously.

- **Stick to the spirit of the rules** People at all organisational levels need to facilitate, support and expect existing rules and regulations about hours of work and rest to be applied.

It is one thing to publicly insist that the rules are followed, but easy to overlook them in order to meet company or operational demands. Your organisational culture is critical here. What is your answer to the following questions?

› In your ship or company, do you feel you can easily ask to stop the job because you are due a rest break? Or don't you need to because your relief is always available?

› How good are your organisation's contingency plans for when a relief is unavailable due to sickness or new priorities?

› Do your organisation's shore managers greet repeated news of operational delays due to rest breaks positively? Do such delays trigger reviews of company manning and work/rest policies?

› Is your organisation's ship manning policy based on a comprehensive and credible workload analysis?

› Does your manning policy include assessment of the new risks and demands created by the automation that was adopted in the attempt to reduce manning requirements?

› Does your organisation live by a fatigue management plan (see panel, *What is a fatigue management plan?*)?

A fatigue management plan is an organisational commitment to avert sleep debt. It is pursued simultaneously on these three levels:

**1. The shipowner/ship manager ensures:**
- Clear communication of ISM Code requirements
- Adequate rest for joining crews before assuming duties
- Adequate time for proper hand-over on crew change
- Voyage length, time in port, length of service, & leave ratios OK
- Good use of time in port for administrative tasks
- Language barriers, social, cultural & religious isolation overcome

**2. The Master ensures:**
- All elements of the shipowner/manager policy met (as above)
- Small crew issues met, eg loneliness, boredom, higher workload
- Adequate shore leave, onboard recreation, and family contact
- Effective work/rest arrangements and napping opportunities
- Potentially hazardous tasks are scheduled for daytime hours
- Crew education and training to recognise and mitigate fatigue
- Creation of open, just culture for reporting & dealing with fatigue
- Rotation of high-demand and low-demand tasks
- Accuracy of individual record keeping of hours rested/worked
- Adequate heating, ventilation, air-conditioning and lighting
- Minimisation of noise and vibration in rest areas
- Healthy lifestyle and diet

**3. The seafarer ensures:**
- Adequate personal sleep arrangements
  - › Aim for deep, uninterrupted sleep 7-8 hours per 24-hour day
  - › Take strategic naps – see panel, *The power of the nap*
  - › Develop pre-sleep routine, eg warm shower, light reading
  - › Ensure dark, quiet, cool sleep area and comfortable bed
  - › Avoid interruptions during extended period of sleep
- Adequate diet and fitness – see panel, *Are you a galley slave?*
  - › Avoid alcohol and caffeine before sleep
  - › Eat regular, well-balanced meals, but eat lightly before bed
  - › Exercise regularly – it increases alertness both on and off duty
- Adequate self-monitoring
  - › Accurately record hours of work and rest
  - › Minimise disturbance of rest/sleep patterns
  - › Take a break between work periods
  - › Get sufficient sleep before high activity periods

*Adapted from ALERT! (2007), with permission*



### Do fatigue management plans work?

Yes. A fatigue management programme was introduced in a Canadian road haulage company in 2002, producing significant savings to the company's top line through reduced lost time and productivity improvements. Over three years:

- The personal injury rate fell by 80%
- The major accident rate fell by 60%
- The staff turnover rate fell by 35%.

*Source: Moore-Ede (2005)*

### Are you a galley slave?

Food is a powerful fatigue management tool. You can help control your fatigue levels by both what you eat and when. Here are the key tips:

- Meals made up largely of carbohydrates facilitate better sleep
- Meals made up largely of protein assist wakefulness and activity
- Regular meal timings help to regulate the human 24-hour cycle
- On night watch, main meals should be eaten before 01.00 hrs
- After night watch, a light snack of carbohydrates should be taken no later than two hours before expected sleep time
- Drinking alcohol before sleep is a bad idea – it may help you to 'drop off', but shortens the deep sleep you really need
- Taking caffeine within 4 hours of sleep is likely to disrupt it. But it can assist nap recovery – see panel, *The power of the nap*

*Adapted from Murphy (2002), with permission of Dir. of Psychology, Aus DoD*

## What's the connection between fatigue & stress?

Fatigue is a normal human response to normal human activity. Similarly, sleep is a normal human response to tiredness. The daily cycle of work/fatigue/sleep is a normal, healthy part of human life. As people pass through this cycle, their level of arousal fluctuates, which in turn helps to determine how alert they can be to their surroundings.

### The power of the nap

Operational seafaring demands – eg the six on/six off watch system – often mean it is not possible to take the ideal 7-8 hour sleep period each 24 hours. In these circumstances, napping becomes a powerful friend. Here is how to get the most out of it:

- The longer the nap, the greater the increase in mood, performance and alertness – but the longer it takes to recover. Always allow a few minutes for the grogginess to clear – up to 30 minutes if the nap has been 2 hours or so
- Naps taken between 04.00 and 06.00 and 14.00 to 16.00 are accompanied by most grogginess on waking – so allow for it
- Afternoon naps have the best chance of repaying some sleep debt since they contain the most Stage 4 sleep
- Naps are best taken before fatigue builds up, rather than after
- Naps should be taken in a comfortable, darkened area free of noise. Noise prevents deeper napping, and reduces its benefit, so ear plugs and eye shades should be considered. Chairs that recline and provide leg support are of most benefit
- Naps of 20-30 minutes provide significant benefit and the least grogginess afterwards. Even naps of 10 minutes are worthwhile
- Caffeine taken just before a 30-minute nap will kick in at wake-up time, assisting recovery to alertness

*Adapted from Murphy (2002), with permission of Dir. of Psychology, Aus DoD*

When people are faced with very few demands, their arousal levels tend to be very low. As a result, their alertness suffers, and they will often feel bored and tired. As the demands around them increase, people become more aroused in order to cope with them. Their alertness levels increase and, unless they are suffering from a severe sleep debt, their feelings of fatigue can disappear. The problem comes if demands go on increasing.

Stress is produced when the demands on people (perceived or real) consistently exceed their ability to meet them. Stress produces a complicated series

# Arousal is good.
# Stress is bad.

One of the first signs of chronic stress is difficulty in sleeping, which can then contribute to the development of sleep debt. The inability of people to repay their sleep debt through stress-induced insomnia can itself become a source of stress. This creates a particularly vicious circle in which stress increases sleep debt which increases stress level, with the result that performance levels decline ever faster.

So, normal fatigue is not stress. However, the inability to deal effectively with fatigue can become a source of stress, as can the sleep debt that results. In addition, stress can increase fatigue by stimulating too much production of adrenalin – the source of the human 'fight or flight' reaction.

## What are the causes of stress?

Stress can be caused by a large number of factors. Some of these factors are work-related while others may belong to the private lives of the person affected.

Seafarers are particularly vulnerable to both sources since their work brings them into contact with many known work-related stressors as well as removing them from their home lives and countries for long periods. The panel, *Common sources of seafarer stress*, summarises the research findings as they relate to seafarers in particular.



of changes in the body's hormone levels and blood chemistry. Over a prolonged period, this can result in a wide range of adverse physical and behavioural changes in people (see panel, *What are the signs and symptoms of stress?*), as well as increased vulnerability to illness. While stress is a common part of human life, it is not the same as arousal, and is always bad.

It is important to realise that all the sources of stress in a person's life tend to add together. For example, a moderate source of stress onboard – such as pain from a muscle injury – can combine with personal worries about marital or financial difficulties to produce severe stress reactions that can mystify fellow crew members or take them by surprise.

## How can stress be reduced?

### By designing it out

As for fatigue, the most powerful approach to dealing with job-related stress is to make the necessary arrangements for stopping it happening in the first place[7]:

- Equipment and materials should be designed to minimise noise and vibration

- Lighting should be designed not only to be adequate for carrying out required tasks, but to facilitate work/rest/sleep cycles so that sleep debt does not build up

- The general arrangements of ships should be designed to support the capabilities, limitations and needs of their crews, and not simply as a result of cargo economics. It is as valid to consider the costs of malfunctioning crews – and the damage they can do – as it is the number of containers a ship can be engineered to carry

- The requirements for ship manning complements, automation and the resulting work procedures need to be specified as a result of comprehensive and thorough workload modelling by designers. This will help to avert the stress of high workload levels, as well as achieve effective work/rest cycles that avoid stress-inducing sleep debt

- Shipping operations and their regulation by classification societies and port authorities should be subject to continuous systemic design review. This will make it possible to find ways of achieving the required standards without over-burdening Masters and crews – either with paperwork or rules and procedures to observe. It will also assist in developing accountability without undue criminalisation (see section on *Making mistakes*, especially on 'just culture')

### By talking about it

It is inevitable that from time to time seafarers will be stressed with external demands and personal worries. It is important that these times are recognised by both the seafarers concerned and their managers – both ashore and afloat.

Whatever the circumstances of the stress experienced, the solution always involves some form of dialogue to reduce or eliminate it. To be effective, this dialogue requires an organisational culture that recognises the problem, and understands the stake that everyone has in solving it. What are the important aspects of this culture?

- **Listening culture** – to ensure that people who are suffering from stress will be noticed, taken seriously and the sources of their stress dealt with, eg via advice, counselling, training or job transfer

- **Learning culture** – to ensure that feedback will be collected and used to influence ongoing refits and maintenance improvements, as well as the design of new ships, equipment, procedures and effective training

- **Open culture** – to ensure that information about organisational issues, intentions, policies, and changes will be communicated early and honestly to employees

- **Reporting culture** – to ensure that seafarers' health concerns can be registered and answered and that any appropriate action will be taken

- **Empathetic culture** – to ensure that[8]:

  › crews are given the means to communicate with their families and friends affordably and easily, eg by internet, subsidised telephone, sufficiently frequent post

  › the frequency of actual contact between seafarers and their families is increased, eg by offering reduced tours of duty, creating more opportunities for partners to sail, improving contact between the company and seafarers' partners, assurance of immediate repatriation in the event of family crisis

  › social isolation is reduced, eg by supporting seafarers who wish to sail with the same crew

Stress is always bad. Design for it. Listen for it. Manage it away.

---

[7] For example, see ABS (2001)



[8] Recommendations from Thomas (2005)

Organisations may wish to consider that the costs of reducing stress via these methods will almost certainly be offset by the increased ease with which they attract seafaring recruits as a result.

## Around the buoys again

The main points covered by this section are as follows.

Fatigue is an inevitable and normal human response to wakeful activity. The onset of fatigue is affected by workload, perceived risk, diet, fitness, the time of day and environmental factors such as light, noise, vibration, temperature and motion.

The only treatment for fatigue is sleep. Sleep needs to last sufficiently long to include several periods of deep sleep and REM (dream) sleep. If not, we build up a 'sleep debt' which causes us to misread situations, overlook key information and fall asleep even when we know it will put us and our colleagues in extreme danger.

Many lessons were learned about the role of fatigue and sleep debt in ship and environmental safety from the 1989 *Exxon Valdez* disaster. However, the same organisational mistakes continue to be made to the present day throughout the industry.

Sleep debt is caused by disruptions to sleep itself – such as loud noise, bright lights, temperature extremes and motion; and by disruption to people's natural daily rhythms. Both causes are especially prevalent in the

---

# D O's

DO insist on a fatigue management plan that is endorsed from the Board downwards. Your company may need to liaise with regulatory bodies, such as port authorities and your Classification Society, in order to ensure their procedures mesh with yours.

DO insist on a review of all other operational procedures in conjunction with your fatigue management plan. You need to ensure that the policies are in harmony with each other. If they are not, your organisation will get behaviour that is too narrowly focused on local problems rather than aimed at averting future problems by reference to the bigger picture.

DO take sleep debt seriously. The Australian Government (2000) found that the decrease in performance of someone who has been awake for 24 hours is equivalent to that associated with a blood alcohol level 25% more than the current (2010) legal UK limit. This makes them seven times more likely to have an accident. Sleep debt develops if people get insufficient deep sleep, which requires them to sleep for 7-8 hours in every 24. If watch systems do not permit this, fatigue can be managed to some extent by diet, physical environment and napping. However, if sleep debt builds up over a week or two, people must be given the opportunity to repay it by at least two normal sleep periods over two or three consecutive days.

DO ensure ship design specifications for lighting, noise, vibration, climate and motion exceed the levels associated with human harm, so that they also meet crew needs for rest and the avoidance of stress. The full needs of seafarers can best be met by a human factors integration plan that accompanies the life of a new project from its earliest stages.

DO develop an organisational culture that supports openness of information and its timely communication between employees at all levels and between crews and their families. Along with design, it is the best way of reducing stress among seafarers.

---

# D O NT's

DON'T assume that fatigue is an inevitable part of seafaring life. People who are tired have accidents. Accidents cost companies seriously large amounts of shareholders' money and seriously large amounts of pain and misery. The STCW and ILO working hours are maximum limits, not recommended norms. It is not normal in any other human profession – let alone a safety-critical one – to work 13 hours a day, every day, for months on end.

DON'T make the mistake that fatigue is simply due to long hours and workload. These factors are certainly direct causes, but other factors help determine the onset of tiredness. These include physical fitness, diet, interest in the task and its perceived riskiness, the time of day, the physical environment (ie light, noise, vibration, motion) and sleep disruption due to stress. All of these need to be addressed in an effective fatigue management plan.

DON'T confuse human arousal with stress. People need to be aroused within certain limits in order to maintain their levels of alertness. However, stress is always bad since it signifies that the person is failing to cope with the demands placed upon them. Stress leads to bodily changes and illness that only make the situation even worse for the person affected.

---

lives of seafarers, who are unique amongst the safety-critical professions. They must spend long, continuous periods of time working, resting and recuperating inside a designed environment whose prime function is to survive a dangerous natural environment over which people have little control.

As a result, design should play a big part in assisting seafarers in the essential task of restorative sleep. However, to do so requires designers to go beyond the limits for lighting, noise, vibration (etc) that must be observed to prevent harm, and pay attention to the lower limits that are relevant to sleep and rest.

Operationally, there are many other things that can be done to address fatigue and avoid sleep debt. Principal among these is the use and support of an effective fatigue management plan. However, the success of such a plan involves all levels of the organisation, and the cooperation of many other parts of the shipping industry – Masters and crews, shipowners and managers, regulators and inspectors. For example, it is entirely counter-productive to shipping safety if port inspections require the attention of fatigued ships' crews during their rest periods.

Similarly, the explicit expectation by boardrooms that their crews observe the hours of work and rest laid down by the regulations must be matched by operational policies that allow them to actually be observed. If there is a policy mismatch, the course of least resistance will be human behaviour that the organisation least wants. Examples are falsified duty logs, people who go to sleep on watch without anyone else around to notice, and fatigue-based accident statistics that do not improve.

Stress is a normal human response to a bad human situation. It leads to damaging physiological changes and occurs when the demands on people consistently exceed their capabilities. Stressors such as constant noise and vibration, domestic, personal and employment worries, social isolation and loneliness can contribute to sleep debt, which turns fatigue itself into a source of stress.

Strategically, stress can be addressed by sensitive, human-centred design of ships, their spaces and their materials.

Operationally, stress can be addressed best by timely communications between those affected, their families and their managers. To do this requires an appropriate organisational culture founded on openness, reporting and learning. Above all, it requires an empathetic culture based on an organisation realising that its profits depend on its safety. And since its safety is created by people who are free from fatigue and stress, reducing these to acceptable levels is an effective investment in its own future.

## Deeper waters

ABS (2001) *Crew Habitability on Ships, American Bureau of Shipping*, Dec 2001

ALERT! (2007) *Time to wake up to the consequences of fatigue*, The International Maritime Human Element Bulletin, The Nautical Institute, Issue No. 13 January 2007

Australian Government (2000) Beyond the Midnight Oil: An Inquiry into Managing Fatigue in Transport, House of Representatives Transport Committee, Australian Government

Calhoun S.R (LT) & Lamb T. (1999) *Human Factors in Ship Design: Preventing and Reducing Shipboard Operator Fatigue*, University of Michigan Department of Naval Architecture and Marine Engineering
U.S. Coast Guard Research Project

HSE (2004) *Work-related stress: a short guide*, Health & Safety Executive

HSE (2006) *Fatigue and Risk Index*: In Nov 2009, the report is at http://www.hse.gov.uk/research/rrpdf/rr446.pdf (in Mar '10)

LUL (2007) *Integration of Human Factors into Systems Development*, London Underground Ltd, Standard 1-217 v. A1, Oct 2007, LUL/WN/00834

MAIB (2009b) *Report on the investigation of the grounding of Antari Near Larne, Northern Ireland 29 June 2008*, Marine Accident Investigation Branch, Carlton House, Carlton Place, Southampton, UK, Report No 7/2009, February 2009

MOD (2008) DefStan 00-250 *Human Factors for Designers of Systems*, Pts 0 - 4, UK Ministry of Defence http://www.dstan.mod.uk (in Mar '10)

Moore-Ede M., Heitmann A., Dawson T. & Guttkuhn R. (2005) *Truckload Driver Accident, Injury and Turnover Rates Reduced by Fatigue Risk-Informed Performance-Based Safety Program.* Transport Canada: Proceedings of the 2005 International Conference on Fatigue Management in Transportation Operations, September 2005, Seattle. http://www.tc.gc.ca/innovation/tdc/publication/ tp14620/h04.htm (in Mar '10)

Murphy P.J. (2002) *Fatigue management during Operations: A Commander's Guide*, Defence Science and Technology Organisation, Australian Department of Defence (Army)

Parker A.W., Hubinger L.M., Green S., Sargaent L. & Boyd R. (1997) *A Survey of the Health, Stress and Fatigue of Australian Seafarers.* Canberra: Australian Maritime Safety Authority

RSSB (2006) *Coping with Shift Work & Fatigue: a good practice guide for drivers*, Rail Safety and Standards Board, London

Smith A., Allen P. & Wadsworth E. (2006) *Seafarer Fatigue: The Cardiff Research Programme*, Centre for Occupational & Health Psychology, Cardiff University

Sutherland, V.J. and Flin, R.H. (1989) *Stress at Sea: A Review of Working Conditions in the Offshore Oil and Fishing Industries*, Work and Stress 3(3): 269–85

Thomas M. (2005) *Lost at Sea and Lost at Home: the Predicament of Seafaring Families*, Seafarers International Research Centre, Cardiff University

Thomas M. & Bailey N. (2006) *Square pegs in round holes? Leave periods and role displacement in UK-based seafaring families*, Work, Employment & Society, Volume 20, No. 1, Sage publications

US DoD (1999) *MIL-STD-1472F Human Engineering Military Specifications and Standards*, US Department of Defense

*Online resources (in Mar '10)*

BBC tools
www.bbc.co.uk/science/humanbody/sleep/

National Sleep Foundation
www.sleepfoundation.org/

Sleep Council
www.sleepcouncil.com/

Talk about sleep
www.talkaboutsleep.com/

Sleep Apnoea Trust
http://www.sleep-apnoea-trust.org/

Working Time Society
http://www.workingtime.org

# Learning and developing

## Learning is normal …

We learn all the time. We can't help it. You are doing it now. We constantly acquire new knowledge, new skills and new attitudes. We learn by aspiring, copying, comparing, interpreting and practising. And as we learn, we change into different people with new capabilities and new learning potential.

Learning is a fundamental survival mechanism of all mammalian species, and humans are particularly good at it. So the question for safety-critical organisations like the maritime industry is not whether people learn, but what they learn – and by what means. The answer to these questions is more – or less – in the control of their managers and employers. As a result, it is less – or more – of a danger to everybody concerned, for without the right guidance, people learn the wrong things.

First, though, let's take a brief look at the nature of learning itself.

## … so, what is learning?

A common, but incorrect, view of learning is that it involves transmitting information from outside the individual to inside their head. This view places emphasis on the skill of the teacher or the appeal of the learning materials, the better for the learner to 'absorb' them.

While instructional skills and content formats are certainly important, learning is an activity exclusively carried out by the learner. No-one else can do it for them, and it doesn't happen by absorption.

> **People are always learning. Organisations just need to make sure it's the right thing.**

Fundamentally, we learn by actively creating meaning for new things in relation to things that already have meaning for us (see panel, *How do people learn?*).

### *Basic principles*

We are best able to incorporate new knowledge, skills and attitudes if these basic principles hold:

- The things we are learning are already almost learned – ie are within our grasp, either as a serial next step or via an analogical leap. Learning serially might involve, for example, learning about a new propulsion system in logical order, step by step, until every part had been covered. Learning by analogy might involve learning about the new system function by function, by comparing and contrasting each function with what is already known about an older propulsion system. Either way, the new material must be easily 'graspable' by the learner.

- We view the things we are learning as intrinsically interesting and rewarding

- We see the point of learning them – ie we understand where the new knowledge or skill will get us

- We aspire to the benefits the learning will bring us – ie we want to be where it will get us

- We trust the source of the learning materials – ie our teachers are credible and earn our respect

### Formal vs. informal learning

Training interventions will be effective if they use the basic principles above. However, learners *always* use them, and in the absence of effective formal training, we informally learn what our colleagues do, what the shortcuts are, what seems to make sense to us, and what behaviours are rewarded. Informal learning may or may not result in safe behaviour. Often, the organisation will not find out until an unsafe behaviour is transformed by a host of other circumstances into injury, loss or worse.

People form attitudes towards their organisation – and the industry as a whole – about the quality (low or high) of the effort to provide them with the information they need. And whatever people learn, they in turn transmit to others, helping to define and maintain the nature of the overall culture to which they belong.

Organisations often claim that *'people are their greatest asset'*. This is perfectly true if the people in question are known to be sharing best practice in knowledge, skills and attitudes that is focused on the organisation's goals. If not, these same people may instead represent an organisational liability of unknown and possibly catastrophic magnitude.

Learning often involves the deliberate investment of significant amounts of time and effort both individually and organisationally. Such is the case for the different, but complementary, activities of formal education and training programmes (see panel, *What's the difference between education and training?*).

Outside formal training activities, learning can seem effortless, automatic and constant. This is the kind of learning that people do in both social and work situations when they simply interact with colleagues, picking up each other's habits, practices, customs, values and techniques.



Whether the context is educational, training, or informal, the underlying process of learning is highly related to that of sense-making (see section on *Making sense of things*). In fact the difference between the two is really a matter of focus (see panel, *What's the difference between learning and sense-making?*).

> When organisations invest in training, they take control of their own future.

### What are the benefits of investment in training?

There are clear career benefits to individuals who participate in their organisation's training and development programmes.

There are also major benefits to the organisation. Here are three:

- **Increased organisational productivity** Newly acquired knowledge, skills and attitudes will be used for the organisation's benefit during subsequent practice. Training courses offer the means for an organisation to ensure that its operational procedures are properly communicated, effectively understood and safely executed. Training also ensures that organisations receive maximum return on their investment in new equipment and all of its expensive functionality.

- **More effective organisational culture** All the time trainees are receiving organisational attention, the organisation will be publicly seen to address job content, methods, tools, teamwork, and interfaces with other seafaring organisations, as well as attitudes to all of these. Together, all these aspects help people to internalise a positive organisational culture which they then re-transmit through their own behaviour and values in practice.

- **Reduced organisational staffing problems** People's career development not only satisfies their own need to make progress, but is of huge strategic benefit to the organisation. This is because people interpret their organisation's investment in them as a clear sign that the organisation values its people and understands the real importance of its investment in them. In turn, these higher-level lessons become known throughout and outside the organisation, improving its staff retention statistics as well as making it easier to attract higher-calibre recruits.

## How to profit from training

## 1. Analyse needs.
## 2. Design content.
## 3. Evaluate results.
## 4. Go to Step 1.

The benefits of organisational investment in learning and development have been recognised for some time by programmes such as the UK's Investors In People (IIP). IIP has been in operation since the early 1990s and is now used in over 50 countries by some 35,000 organisations. Independent reports[1] confirm the benefits described above – mainly through the greater focus and engagement of staff on business performance. In particular, the overall IIP programme has been found to set up a 'chain of impact' that has measurable positive effects on financial performance.

### What's involved in training investment?

Some organisations may consider their investment in staff learning and development as part of an overall business improvement programme. Such organisations are encouraged to contact initiatives such as IIP[2].

Good practice in learning and development hinges on three key organisational activities: training needs analysis, training design and delivery, and training evaluation. Here, we look at the main points for each of these three activities.

*Training needs analysis*

Training needs analysis (TNA) should be carried out routinely as an integral part of everyone's performance appraisal process. In addition, it should be used by the organisation's trainers, designers and equipment buyers to provide timely support for new equipment or work processes. TNA is usually carried out in three phases:

- **Phase 1: Task identification** – in which a list of tasks is agreed, some or all of which may be new if a novel system is being introduced. Each task is described in terms of its operational circumstances, procedures and required performance standard. It is often helpful to rate each task in terms of its difficulty, importance and frequency. This first phase of TNA requires the contribution of subject matter experts.

- **Phase 2: Training gap identification** – in which a set of training objectives are produced that, if met, will eliminate the gap between current knowledge, skills and attitudes and those required. This second phase of TNA often requires the contribution of training specialists.

- **Phase 3: Training solution identification** – in which the most cost-effective training option is selected from the range of available possibilities. This third phase of TNA requires contributions from subject matter experts, training, technology and the organisation's financial team. The panel, *Training aids: what are the options?* gives further guidance.

---

[1] Cranfield School of Management (2008)

[2] http://www.investorsinpeople.co.uk (in Mar '10)

Here are four training options for different situations and budgets.

### High-fidelity simulation
*Description* Specialist computer equipment that realistically simulates the task environment and allows realistic interaction.
*Pros* Rare and dangerous tasks, procedures and drills can be safely and easily practised in addition to routine ones; supports very high transfer of training to operational settings; permits thorough training and certification procedures.
*Cons* Expensive to create and maintain; total task simulation is often overwhelming to newer trainees.

### Computer-based training
*Description* Uses standard personal computers to deliver prepared multi-media materials from local software packages or web servers.
*Pros* Good at explaining complex material through animated or interactive diagrams and models; supports self-paced learning; highly portable for remote, opportunistic use; supports moderate levels of testing and training management. Known to be popular with seafarers, as long as time is made available (Ellis et al, 2005).
*Cons* High development costs that increase with content complexity and/or frequent revision; requires trainee computer literacy, motivation and discipline; inappropriate if Q&A needed.

### Embedded training
*Description* Software that runs on operational equipment in the field to provide user guidance or training, eg via context-sensitive help or display stimulation with artificial signals for training.
*Pros* Reduces dependence on manuals; increases productivity via on-line support; utilises real equipment in training mode.
*Cons* Requires sufficient user understanding to make help meaningful; requires trainee to take more effective control of their learning due to reduced opportunity for training feedback.

### Chalk and talk
*Description* Traditional classroom courses and workshops, supported by models, presentation tools and audio-visual aids.
*Pros* Low cost; extended contact with other trainees and subject matter experts; supports Q&A, self-expression and free discussion.
*Cons* Not self-paced; does not suit some learning styles; does not give realistic representation of operational life.

*Based on material in RSSB (2008), reproduced with permission*



---

## *Training design and delivery*

Once the training objectives have been identified and the mix of training solutions decided, training designers need to develop the content, format and sequencing of the training materials that will facilitate the most efficient learning. To achieve this, the following five aspects of design need to be addressed:

- **Learner engagement**

   Training designers need to pay full attention to the five learning principles set out on the first page of this section. If trainees are not engaged by the material, or do not feel it is in their interests to pay attention to it, a great deal of effort, time and investment cost will be wasted.

- **Knowledge training** Materials aimed at increasing understanding of concepts and their relationships will benefit from sequencing. Research[3] recommends starting with the simple presentation of single concepts, before progressing through rules that combine concepts, to more complex problem solving involving those rules. Training designers need to ensure that examples are selected to illustrate different instances, generalisations and exceptions. The materials should also support exploration by the trainees according to their preferred learning style.

[3] Gagné, Briggs & Wager (1992)

---

> **Full simulation allows whole task coverage plus safe practice in rare circumstances – but it's not for novices.**

- **Skills training** Skills appear to be developed in three stages[4]:

   › *Thinking* – in which the required performance is verbalised and mentally rehearsed. Training designers must provide the means for clear explanations of the relevant principles, objectives and techniques via models, demonstrations and discussions.

   › *Doing* – in which the required performance becomes increasingly fluid and error-free. Training designers should consider if the task can be divided into discrete sections, and if so, arrange for a part task approach to simplify the learning task. If the task cannot easily be subdivided, training designers should arrange for trainees to be able to engage with increasingly detailed approximations of the task as a whole.

   › *Tuning* – in which the required performance becomes more automatic and trainees are able to work more efficiently, anticipate the future better, and seem to have more time for decision making. Training designers can use this stage to introduce complexity in the form of malfunctions or some form of degraded working – especially effective if a simulator is being used. Simulators also make it easy to support 'overtraining'. Here, training is allowed to proceed beyond the required criterion for certification, eg through repeated

[4] Following Anderson (1982)

practice. An alternative overtraining approach is 'above real time' training where trainees carry out the task at speeds greater than they will encounter in real life. The advantage of these overtraining methods is that they can increase resistance of important procedures to fatigue and stress in actual operational settings.

- **Trainee feedback** People learn through knowing how they have done. They are then able to know how to adjust their performance to make progress towards the required standard. Training designers need to plan for a number of different kinds of feedback to provide comprehensive learning support. These kinds of feedback are:

  › *What's happening?* Explanations of the behaviour and function of task objects and relationships

  › *What should I be doing?* Explanations of the relevant rules and how they should have been applied by the trainee

  › *How did I do?* Debrief of the trainee's performance in specific scenarios and explanations of alternative actions and interpretations

  › *How am I doing overall?* Review of the trainee's overall performance across different scenarios and comparison with the required certification standard

- **Skill fade** This refers to the tendency for skills to decay over time. Research[5] has identified a wide range of factors that are known to influence skill fade. The following all help training designers to increase resistance to skill fade:

› Higher similarity between the training and operational contexts (eg in terms of environmental characteristics, time demands, operator's mood state)

› Higher internal connectivity of the material, eg each step of a procedure carries with it a good 'reminding' clue for the next step

› More opportunity to rehearse the training material

› Functional explanations as well as actual practice for more complex tasks

› Feedback in summary form after a series of practice sessions (rather than after every session)

› Gradually phasing out feedback to the learner as performance improves

› Expecting and receiving a performance evaluation test

› Higher-aptitude trainees

› Fewer numbers of task steps

› Less rigid sequences of task steps

› Fewer mental processing and/or physical demands for each task step

### Training evaluation

Just as trainees can only learn effectively if they receive performance feedback, so organisations can only optimise their training investment strategy if they can evaluate the impact of the training they have paid for.

> **Proper evaluation means going deep.**



Four levels of evaluation are possible, although very often organisations never get much deeper than the first level. The panel, *Training evaluation: how deep can you go?* summarises the four levels. In practice, organisations may find it difficult to evaluate beyond the first level for several reasons:

[5] Summarised and developed in Gregory Harland Ltd (1999)

- It may be difficult to measure job performance after trainees return to operations, eg because they are dispersed too widely or because local factors would interfere with the results

- The gap between training and job may be too long to be able to make improvements to the training content – so there is little point

- There may be organisational resistance to post-training data collection – due to management fears about what operational performance results might reveal, and how this might reflect on managers, rather than on the training

- In challenging financial times there may not be the budget for it

In the absence of deeper levels of evaluation, the main problems are that:

- The organisation has little idea about the return on its training investment – or how to re-direct it in future

- The organisation can mislead itself about the true extent of the expertise available to it – a situation which may only come to light in unusual or emergency conditions, ie exactly when the benefit of training is needed

In practice, these problems can be offset by:

- Using part of each training course to help trainees gain better insight into their own learning (learning to learn)

- Ensuring regular in-course testing is used – especially that which requires trainees to recall material rather than recognise it. Open-ended questions are far better learning revision tools than multiple-choice questions for this reason

- Ensuring that skills training courses use tests based on increasingly closer approximations to the whole operational task. These permit more accurate indicators of later job performance compared to part-task assessments

## DO's

DO be aware that people learn things all the time and that most of what they learn comes from the people they work with. Organisations can be sure that people learn the right things by ensuring that everyone is trained properly.

DO consider a competence development framework such as Teekay's SCOPE (Seafarer Competence for Operational Excellence), Intertanko's TOTS (Tanker Officer Training Standard) or SIGGTO for your organisation. People don't learn everything they need to carry out your organisation's business safely and efficiently simply though exposure to the job. Experience is essential, but so is learning to do the right thing in the first place.

DO be clear that good trainers are people who understand how students are viewing things and can use this information to re-structure training materials. Subject matter expertise is necessary, but not sufficient to make someone an effective trainer.

DO carry out training needs analysis, training design and outcome evaluation for all staff as a continuous organisational improvement process. It's the best way of maximising the return on investment, leading to increased productivity, a safer organisational culture, and reduced recruitment and retention problems.

## DONT's

DON'T assume that one training type fits all. Trainees need different kinds of training and refresher support depending on their level of expertise (eg novice vs advanced), and on what they are learning (eg skills vs knowledge).

DON'T be satisfied with training evaluation that stops after assessing trainee satisfaction. Deeper levels of evaluation (eg against course objectives, and job and organisational performance) will deliver much better information about return on training investment and how to redirect future training spend. It will also reassure senior management that the expertise needed by the organisation is actually available to it.

### Around the buoys again

The main points covered by this section are as follows.

Learning is a fundamental human process that has much in common with sense-making. We learn by actively creating meaning for new things in relation to things that already have meaning for us. We do it all the time and do it best and most effortlessly when we are engaged by the material and understand how it is in our interests to be engaged in this way.

Learning takes place formally in an educational or training context, or else informally and socially alongside other people, such as crew members. Whatever the arrangements for learning within an organisation, people will learn. While people – and what they know – can be an organisation's best asset, they will only be so if they are known to be focused on planned organisational goals via shared best practice. If the organisation has not made arrangements for the focused learning and development of its staff, its people may represent an unknown and potentially catastrophic liability and risk to the organisation, rather than an asset.

The benefits to an organisation of investing in the training and development of its staff include increased productivity, a more effective organisational culture and reduced staffing problems. Organisations can most effectively invest in training and development of staff by:

- Ensuring training needs analysis is carried out as part of its performance appraisal process or when new equipment is planned

- Paying attention to training design so that learner engagement is assured

- Carrying out training evaluation sufficiently well to understand how to fine-tune its future training investment in line with its future business goals

The panel, *How much has your company learned about training?* indicates potential areas for attention.

## Deeper waters

Anderson J.R. (1982) *Acquisition of cognitive skill.* Psychological Review, 89, 369-406

Cranfield School of Management (2008) *Impact of Investors in People on People Management Practices and*

*Firm Performance*

Ellis N., Sampson H., Aguado J.C., Baylon A., Del Rosario L., Lim Y.F. & Veiga, J. (2005) *What Seafarers think of CBT*, Seafarers International Research Centre Cardiff University http://www.sirc.cf.ac.uk/pdf/CBT%20Report.pdf (in Mar '10)

Gagné R.M., Briggs L.J. & Wager W.W. (1992) *Principles of Instructional Design*, Holt, Rinehart & Winston

Gregory Harland Ltd (1999) *Development of a skill fade model*, GHL/CHS/SkillFade/Deliverables/FinalReport/ Volume1/v3.0, Centre for Human Sciences, DERA

Investors In People (IIP) http://www.investorsinpeople.co.uk (in Mar '10)

Maturana H.M. & Varela F.J. (1980) *Autopoeisis and Cognition: The Realization of the Living*, Dordrecht: D. Reidel Vol 42 Boston Studies in the Philosophy of Science

Pask G. (1976) *Conversation Theory*, Applications in Education and Epistemology, Elsevier

RSSB (2008) *Understanding Human Factors – a guide for the railway industry*, Rail Safety and Standards Board, Angel Square, 1 Torrens Street, London EC1V 1NY. http://www.rssb.co.uk/expertise/human_factors/ human_factors_good_practices_guide.asp (in Mar '10)

# Working with others

### In what ways do we work with others?

When it comes to working with others, the jobs of most seafarers fall into two different sorts of activity. The distinction rests on whether the goals of the activity are individual and independent, or else team-based and shared:

*Working with individuals and in teams requires different sets of skills.*

- **Working with individuals** Here, individuals with independent goals must work with each other to trade information and evaluate its meaning. The resulting decision – arising from, say, a selection interview – will affect the goals of both. The same applies to two people in a job appraisal interview or other formal staff discussion, between accident investigators and witnesses, or between different parties who are in negotiation with each other. In all of these cases, people need sets of interaction skills that will best serve their own, individual goals.

- **Working in teams** In a team task, people must work with each other in mutually supportive ways to achieve a shared goal. Many seafaring jobs require people to work with each other as team members, each of whom contributes their effort to an objective that is bigger than any one of them. In these situations, people need skills that permit not just effective interaction between people, but good teamwork.

Whether people need to work with each other as individuals or as team members, they need sets of social interaction skills over and above whatever technical skills they need to do their job. In this section we explore what these individual and team interaction skills are, how they are different and what can go wrong.

### How can individuals get the best out of each other?

There are many reasons why people need to engage with each other as individuals. Three common seafaring reasons stem from:

- **The need to assess people**, eg when undertaking selection, job appraisals and incident debriefs

- **The need to confront a difficult issue**, eg when giving someone bad news about their family, or disciplining or sacking someone

- **The need to negotiate**, eg when resolving a disagreement with other crew members or agreeing a new labour convention between different nationalities

Let's examine good practice in each of these areas.

### Getting the most out of assessing others

Whether the purpose is selection, appraisal or incident investigation, assessing others usually involves eliciting information from them and making judgments about the information received.

The most common way of eliciting information is the interview. You'll find information on conducting interviews efficiently and fairly in the panel, *What makes a good interview?*

One of the main problems that affects our assessment of others is that it is easy to fall victim to one or another judgmental biases. We are naturally biased in how we experience the world for a great many reasons (see section on *Making sense of things*). The panel, *Without fear or favour: natural biases to avoid*, summarises the most well-known biases. These biases are a lot easier to guard against just by knowing what they are. They are also countered by insisting on evidence-based judgments and assessments from multiple sources including peers and subordinates.

### Coping with difficult conversations

Sooner or later in our lives, most of us are confronted with the task of having to discuss a difficult matter with a friend or colleague. Examples include a supervisor who needs to address someone's bad performance, a Master who needs to give bad news to the bereaved partner of a crew member, or crew members who are in serious dispute with one another. Perhaps surprisingly, research has shown that there are three basic similarities underlying all such conversations – even though they might be about different topics. Here they are[1]:

- **The situation is always more complicated than it looks**
  Quite often, we assume we know all there is to know about another person or situation. We therefore think the

[1] According to Stone et al (2000)

challenge is to get our own message across, or to get the other person to admit their mistake and take the blame. The reality is that there are always two sides to the story, and that both sides will have made assumptions that usually need to be corrected. The key objective is therefore to understand all perspectives and how they have interacted to produce the present situation.

> **Sooner or later, people will find themselves in a difficult conversation.**

- **The situation always involves emotions** By their very nature, difficult conversations always involve emotion. Very often, we try to avoid talking about our own and other people's feelings, or else confuse our feelings with the issue at hand. The trick is to acknowledge and include feelings without allowing them to determine the response that the situation needs. Sometimes, feelings on both sides may have to be properly exposed before they can then be set aside in order to find a way forward.

- **The situation always threatens our sense of who we are** When faced with a difficult issue, such as a judgment that we have performed badly, we often feel that something fundamental about the kind of person we are is being challenged. This makes us defend an image of ourselves which we have usually over-simplified into black or white. However, if you can cultivate a more complex (and therefore more realistic) self-image, you are much more able to achieve a balanced view of the impact of the threatening issues you are facing.

### A better way to negotiate

There is a common view of negotiation that assumes there is a cake of pre-determined size. In this view, the successful negotiator is the one who ends up with more cake than the other. It follows that negotiation is a win-lose game that requires assertiveness and manipulation aimed at overpowering the other side with cleverness and dominating force or else intransigence and attrition.

Negotiation is commonly confused with the kind of marketplace haggling that occurs all over the world. This bargaining behaviour involves each side taking positions (usually ridiculous to start with) and then giving them up as they move towards agreement. The problem with this 'positional bargaining' is that it can lead to people defending positions that may have little to do with the real issues. The process can also be very time consuming, as people wait to be dislodged from their positions and deploy delaying tactics. Furthermore, it can generate long-term feelings of bitterness in the losing side that may damage future interactions.

However, effective negotiators have learned to move away from positional bargaining. For them, negotiation is not a battle over the size of pre-existing cake portions, but more a creative process in which the cake is baked to order. In this way, everyone ends up with the piece of cake they need. Effective negotiation does not involve successively taking and then giving up positions, but should instead be guided by the following four principles[2]:

- **Don't confuse feelings with problems** Negotiation always involves emotion since we tend to feel passionate about problems that require negotiation to resolve them. Emotion has to be acknowledged but not allowed to become a barrier to the real problems requiring resolution. It helps to talk about your own feelings, but never about the other party's: you can't know what they feel, although it is always helpful to acknowledge what they say about their feelings. Listen to them, since it will help prevent you from confusing your fears with their intentions. Knowing their perceptions and values helps you to ensure your proposals are consistent with where they want to be. As a negotiator you need to remember that you can be as tough as you like on the problems you are tackling, but being tough on people just causes defensiveness, retaliation and intransigence.

- **Explore objectives, not positions** We very often confuse the position we want to defend (eg *"I want 10 consecutive off-duty hours"*) with the outcome we are looking for (eg *"I need to have a enough sleep"*). If as a negotiator you keep asking why? and why not?, you will lead the other party towards their real objectives and away from territorial claims. This tactic also tends to expose the range of interests and objectives that the other party has: there

is rarely only one. Another useful tactic is to state the problems you have, not the position you want to defend or aspire to. If both sides adopt this tactic, it will keep you both open to emergent ideas that may be better.

- **Create new options** It is often useful for both parties to set aside time – off the record – to brainstorm as wide a range of options as possible. You should pay attention to any emerging ideas that help you and the other party dovetail your objectives and differences. The result is often a solution that benefits everybody.

- **Agree independent arbitration** It can help enormously if you and the other party are able to agree up front on what you will do if you become entrenched. Decisions on standards, procedures, and a review process by an independent body mean that in a last resort, you can both defer to a third party without one being seen to give in to the other. This works not just as a fail-safe mechanism, but may help prevent entrenchment – just because it exists.

## How can team members work effectively?

### What is a team?

A team is more than a group. While a group may be united by a common location (eg a group of bystanders), or common interests (eg members of a club), a team is united by a common goal, with each member having a defined role to play in achieving it.

This means that each team member must have not only the technical skills to carry out their role, but the

---

[2] According to Fisher et al (1992)

Negotiation is not about winning or losing – it's about creating.

necessary team skills to carry out the role in concert with other team members.

### What are team skills?

Research over many years[3] in a number of different safety-critical industries has revealed five main types of team skill that are essential to team effectiveness. They are as follows[4]:

- **Team leadership** This includes motivating, directing and coordinating team member activities, and assessing and developing team members' knowledge and skills. Good team leaders clarify team roles and performance expectations and engage team members in planning and feedback sessions. They also spend time synchronising individual contributions and seeking information that affects overall team performance.

- **Mutual monitoring** This is concerned with the ability of team members to monitor each other's performance within a common understanding of the constraints and opportunities of the environment in which they must work. Team members who are good at mutual monitoring identify mistakes in their colleagues' actions and provide feedback that helps them to correct themselves.

- **Back-up behaviour** This refers to the ability of team members to understand each other's tasks and responsibilities sufficiently well that they can anticipate problems (eg unacceptably high workload) in each other's tasks and even take over if necessary. Team members who are skilled in back-up behaviour, work continually to avoid problems for their colleagues or take some of the load, since they know that failure to do so will lead to problems for the whole team.

- **Adaptability** This refers to the ability of team members to respond to continuous changes in the environment that affect their plans. Adaptable teams can identify external changes, understand their implications and develop new plans accordingly. They can also create new and better ways to accomplish routine tasks while remaining vigilant about the impact of such procedural changes on their safety.

- **Team orientation** This refers to the degree to which team members are able to see themselves as team members with a common goal, rather than individuals with independent goals. Team members who are highly team oriented are very receptive to the suggestions of their colleagues. They also involve each other in setting goals, and then choosing strategies and sharing the information needed to achieve them.

> **There are five distinct team skills … and three types of team glue.**

People need to use all of these five types of team skill if they are to function as an effective team. However, to assure success, they must also employ three types of 'team glue'[5]. This glue serves to keep team members together through updates on their progress and performance as they carry out their roles.

The three types of 'glue' are:

- **Similar mental models** – so that team members have an agreed understanding of each other's situations and responsibilities, and how they each contribute to team goals and strategies

- **Mutual trust** – so that each team member feels that their actions, misgivings and mistakes will be responded to efficiently and constructively with due regard to overall team goals

- **Effective communication** – so that messages between team members are delivered with as much completeness and certainty as possible within the prevailing conditions (see the section *Communicating with others*)

Let's see what happens when these team skills and coordinating mechanisms are absent.

---

[3] Much of it by Salas and his colleagues – see Salas et al (2008)
[4] Summarised from Salas (2005), with permission

[5] Also based on Salas et al (2005)

## Case study: A bridge too near[6]

At 08.00 hrs on 7 Nov 2007, *Cosco Busan*, a fully loaded 900-foot container ship slipped her berth in San Francisco harbour, bound for South Korea. Visibility was bad. In fact from the bridge, the bow of the ship disappeared at times into the swirling fog. But the port was still open, and the Pilot now at *Cosco Busan's* con had 26 years experience of navigating the San Francisco Bay waters. He had checked the winds and tides, tuned the radars and set them to the range he liked to work with. He steered the big ship up the navigation channel towards San Francisco's Bay Bridge, with an assist tug trailing off her stern. His plan required a course change to port, just before Yerba Buena Island, and then another turn to starboard to take the ship through the centre of the bridge span between Delta and Echo Towers.

With him on the bridge were the Master, the Third Officer and the helmsman. The Bosun was on the bow and the Second Officer was on the stern. With the exception of the Pilot, the entire crew was Chinese. They had all joined the ship following its change of ownership just two weeks previously for the crossing from South Korea to San Francisco. The crew were all new to each other, new to the ship and new to San Francisco. They had spent their first voyage over the previous two weeks both operating, and learning to operate, the ship. Their operations had been supervised, as they sailed, by the company port Captain, a superintendent engineer, and a chief engineer. With only these three to turn to with questions about the ship, the crew's preoccupation with learning company procedures, practising essential drills, and locating

or assembling vessel documentation allowed them little time to focus on training exclusively. Now as they started the voyage back to South Korea, they all still had some way to go before they could function as the team they needed to be.

At 08.30, just half an hour into her voyage, *Cosco Busan* struck Delta Tower of the Bay Bridge. The collision ripped a gash 212 feet long, 10 feet high and 8 feet deep along her port side, rupturing ballast and bunker oil tanks. The ship would lose revenues for six weeks while repairs could be carried out at a direct cost of US$2.1 million. Although the seismometers on the bridge quickly confirmed to local authorities that there was no earthquake in progress, it was necessary to consider closing the entire bridge. In the event, it was kept open, although US$1.5 million would be needed later to repair the damage to Delta Tower.

After striking the support tower, the Pilot correctly decided to take the ship to anchorage two miles beyond the bridge to assess the damage. Unfortunately, as she sailed she leaked 53,000 gallons of fuel oil into the bay, which eventually affected 26 miles of shoreline and closed 27 public beaches. The whole Bay Area was closed to fishing for three weeks. 3,000 birds from 50 species died. The final cost for the environmental clean-up was US$70 million. Two years later, the ship manager agreed to pay a penalty of US$10 million to the US Department of Justice. The legal costs are unknown.

In examining the circumstances of this US$100 million disaster, the investigation team naturally paid particular attention to what happened on *Cosco Busan's* bridge that

morning. The report found that the cocktail of 10 prescription drugs being taken by the Pilot had degraded his mental abilities sufficiently to account for the series of navigation errors that led up to the collision. Two other official primary causes were found. These were that there had been ineffective communications between the Master and Pilot both prior to departure and during the accident voyage, and that the Master's oversight of the Pilot's performance and the vessel's progress had been ineffective[7].

In the period leading up to the day of the accident, the contributing causes were found to include the failure of the ship manager to adequately train the crew and the failure of the US Coastguard to adequately respond to the Pilot's medical circumstances – all of which had been reported to them by the Pilot.

In July 2009, the Pilot made US history when he became the first to receive a prison sentence as result of carrying out his job. He got 10 months for misdemeanour charges, causing pollution and killing migrating seabirds.

What were the team issues here?

The US accident investigation report reveals that the team failed in all areas known to drive effective team performance as outlined above. On the next pages we take a closer look at how this happened.

---

[6] Based on NTSB (2009) with further interpretation by the authors

[7] In fact, one of the investigating team published a dissent, arguing that this should be relegated to a contributing cause due to the primacy of the Pilot's role throughout the incident.

According to *Cosco Busan's* written Safety Management System (SMS), there was no ambiguity about who was in charge. The SMS stated that the Pilot *'acts only as an advisor'*. In practice there was considerable leadership ambiguity – and this was reflected by the dissenting voice on the accident investigation team (see footnote, previous page).

The fact was that none of the Chinese crew had any experience of the Bay Area and the Pilot was an expert. In addition, the Master reported an adversarial 'coldness' on the part of the Pilot from first contact. Whether or not this stemmed from ethnic differences, the Chinese Master – and everyone else – felt disinclined to challenge any part of the Pilot's behaviour over the next half hour. As the ship readied for departure in very poor visibility, there was just one worried comment. It was uttered as an aside by one of the ship's crew in the ship's language – Mandarin – and not acted on by anyone.

There was no meeting of minds between the Pilot and Master. No-one briefed and no-one asked questions about the voyage plan or the challenges of the fog, the planned course changes, hazards or speeds. There was no discussion of the status, workings or use of any of the electronic navigation equipment. Nor was there discussion of the plans for the deployment of the tug.

> ## Together, the Pilot, crew and management fell short in every area known to be essential to effective teamwork.

Not only was there unspoken confusion about who was leader, but neither candidate for the job displayed any of the signs of effective leadership, including motivating, involving, planning or consulting the other team members. Without an agreed plan, mutual monitoring became a matter of assumption and guesswork.

With little possibility for mutual monitoring, and an inadequate relationship between the Pilot and bridge crew based on unspoken assumption, there was no stomach for effective backup behaviour.

Eight minutes before the collision, there was a curious exchange between the Master and Pilot about the meaning of standard symbols on a standard chart of the area that the Pilot knew well. In other circumstances the crew might have been alerted to the Pilot's degraded performance problem. But their deferral to the authority and demeanour of the Pilot was too powerful and no intervention was made (see panel, *Deferring to authority: culture – or basic human nature?*)

Three minutes before the collision, there was another missed opportunity for team backup when the Pilot became confused over the ship's heading during a radio discussion with port control. Again, the opportunity for challenge and intervention came and went.



---

### Deferring to authority: culture – or basic human nature?

It is certainly the case that cultures differ in their attitude to authority. Lewis (2006) says that Americans tend to be individualistic and likely to take decisions without reference to others, while the Chinese have a more group-centred culture where inequalities and obedience are both expected and desired.

But we also need to guard against stereotypes. In all human societies it is usually highly beneficial to defer to authority since this is where the knowledge and wisdom often resides. It is often a short-cut to our own survival to simply obey someone who we see as a credible expert. This tendency is so ingrained in humans that it is often enough to simply display the symbols of authority for people to obey the most outrageous instructions. In a series of highly realistic experiments in the 1960s, US psychologist Stanley Milgram showed that normal, healthy Americans are not immune to the power of mere symbols of authority. Investigating some of the social processes that played their part in Nazi excesses during World War II, Milgram persuaded his US experimental subjects to apparently deliver severe pain to innocent people via near 'fatal' electric shocks. Although many subjects experienced extreme anguish, they still carried on with their tasks as directed by the authority figure – the white coated experimenter – who they assumed would take responsibility.

Being aware of our natural tendency to defer to authority is a big help in defending against doing so where we shouldn't. Learning to be an effective team member addresses this explicitly in courses aimed at teaching Bridge or Engine Room Resource Management. Cialdini (2009) says that our defences can also be strengthened in situations such as the one the Master of *Cosco Busan* was in by always being ready with two questions:

- **Is this authority really an expert?** This question directs attention away from symbols and towards proper evidence of authority.
- **How much trust should we be placing in this expert?** This question encourages continuous scrutiny of credibility.

*Cosco Busan's* Pilot would have passed the first question. Had the second been asked as part of a healthier team process, it might well have resulted in an effective intervention when the Pilot showed confusion over the electronic maps and ship's headings.

*Sources: Milgram (1974), Lewis (2006) and Cialdini (2009)*

The crew did not know each other's capabilities and limitations, or the ship's, or how their new employer expected them to operate it, or how to deal with uncommunicative Western pilots. The supervised operations that had been possible over the previous two weeks had made it impossible to observe the SMS completely: it was only in English, the agreed ship language was Mandarin and some crew had no English.

No-one had received any training in passage planning, bridge team management or cultural difference issues. If the crew had been mixed, the ship management company would have provided – at some stage – training about cultural differences with respect to authority and power relations. But because the crew were all Chinese, no plans were in place to do this – a policy which overlooked the crew's need to deal with port authorities and pilots.

The NTSB conclusion that the primary cause of the accident was the medical condition of the Pilot is clearly right. What is equally clear is that there would have been an unremarkable, unreported and safe outcome had the Pilot and bridge crew functioned as a unified team according to the principles of effective teamwork outlined in this section. Countless incidents like the one involving the *Cosco Busan* are prevented every day by the teams that do function well.

## DO's

DO get the best out of interviews by proper preparation, appropriate conduct and awareness of natural biases that can affect your judgment.

DO consider how you can assess the level of teamworking in your crew or organisation. Perhaps it is included in your company's competency framework. If not, you might consider taking a closer look at other approaches. A process for diagnosing teamworking in UK rail organisations (but with generic value) can be found in RSSB (2004).

DO insist on training in teamworking (eg BRM) from your organisation. It is quite different from the technical skills and knowledge you need, it is learnable, and it is essential to safe and economic ship operations. For more practical advice in this area, see the MCA Guide, *Leading for Safety*.

DO insist on cultural difference training from your organisation. It goes hand in hand with teamwork training.

## DONT's

DON'T avoid difficult conversations. They are necessary and there are good ways to prepare yourself for them.

DON'T make the mistake that negotiation is about winning or losing. It is an opportunity for both sides to create something that works for everybody.

## Around the buoys again

The main points covered by this section are as follows.

Working with others sometimes involves interactions with other individuals who have independent goals and sometimes with other team members who all share the same goal.

Some of the ways in which people work outside of teams include assessment (eg selection and appraisal), confronting difficult issues (eg bereavement and discipline) and negotiating with other parties (eg dispute resolution and new ways of working).

All of these ways are vulnerable to several types of natural biases (such as the halo/horns effect) which need to be guarded against if our dealings with each other are to be fair and reasonable. Many of these vulnerabilities arise from making assumptions that turn out to be too simple or just ill-informed. We like to make assumptions because it saves us time. However, if they are wrong, our assumptions will end up taking even more of our time and lead to bad or even catastrophic decisions. It follows that part of our interactions with each other – whatever their purpose – should always involve identifying and checking these assumptions.

Often, working with others involves us operating as a member of a team. A team is more than a group. While a group may be united by a common location (eg a group of bystanders), or common interests (eg members of a club), a team is united by a common goal, with each member having a defined role to play in achieving it.

Teamwork requires a unique set of skills and practices to be effective, and identifying these has been the subject of a lot of research over the past 20 years or so. The results show that we need to have skills in leading and motivating others, monitoring what each other does, backing up our colleagues, helping the whole team to adapt to changing demands and being receptive to each other's suggestions. Furthermore, these skills need to be all 'glued together' by similar mental models of the team situation, mutual trust and effective communication between team members.

All of these skills are additional to our technical job knowledge and abilities and, just like their technical counterparts, are all trainable.

**Deeper waters**


Cialdini R.B. (2009) *Influence: Science and practice*, Pearson International Edition, Fifth Edition

Fisher R., Ury W. & Patton B. (1992) *Getting to Yes*, 2nd Edition, Random House Business Books

Lewis R.D. (2006) *When Cultures Collide: managing successfully across cultures*, Nicholas Brealey Publishing.

MCA, *Leading for Safety: a practical guide for leaders in the Maritime Industry*, Maritime and Coastguard Agency, MCA 140

Milgram S. (1974) *Obedience to authority: An experimental view*. Harper & Row

NTSB (2009) *Allision of Hong Kong, Registered Containership M/V Cosco Busan with the Delta Tower of the San Francisco–Oakland Bay Bridge San Francisco, California, November 7, 2007*, National Transportation Safety Board, NTSB/MAR-09/01, PB2009-916401

RSSB (2004) *Teamworking in the railway industry: The Journey Guide*. Toolset produced for the Rail Safety and Standards Board by Gregory Harland Ltd http://www.rssb.co.uk/pdf/reports/research/ Teamworking%20in%20the%20railway%20industry%20 -%20The%20Journey%20Guide.pdf (in Mar '10)

RSSB (2008) *Understanding Human Factors – a guide for the railway industry*, Rail Safety and Standards Board, Angel Square, 1 Torrens Street, London EC1V 1NY. http://www.rssb.co.uk/expertise/human_factors/ human_factors_good_practices_guide.asp (in Mar '10)

Salas E., Sims D.E. & Burke C.S. (2005) *Is there a big five in teamwork?* Small Group Research, 36, 155

Salas E., Cooke N.J. & Rosen M.A. (2008) *On teams, teamwork and team performance: Discoveries and developments*. Human Factors, 50, 3, pp. 540-547

Stone D., Patton B. & Heen S, (2000) *Difficult Conversations*, Penguin Books

# Communicating with others

## What is communication?

It is rather easy to be tempted by the engineering approach to this question. In this view, a transmitter encodes a signal in a carrier and transmits it over some medium to a receiver, which decodes the signal from the carrier. To an engineer, a communication is successful if the signal at the receiving end has the same content as at the start, and is strong enough to be distinguishable from the noise (eg static) encountered along the way.

Communication engineers quite naturally focus on technologies to send and preserve signals over a range of distances. These technologies have been extremely successful. They have given us telephones, very long-range short-wave radio, crystal-clear VHF and FM radio, high bandwidth media for realtime data transmission over both vast distances (eg fibre optics) and short range (eg bluetooth and wifi). Satellite and digital media for the high-quality transmission of radar, sonar, navigation, financial and cargo information have transformed the shipping industry and largely enabled its globalisation.

Unfortunately, achieving good 'signal-to-noise ratios' for successful human to human communication is rather more complicated than the problem facing communication engineers. This is because for humans,

signals and noise are relative concepts, not absolutes: what is a signal for one person may simply be noise for another (the later panel, *Stirred, but not shaken*, gives an example of this). Further complexity arises because people don't actually pass meanings to each other. Instead, they use the signals from others to construct meaning for themselves based on what they already know, expect, and are able to attend to (see section on *Making sense of things*).

This is important to understand. When two skilled speakers are in face-to face-discussion with each other, communication is so fast that it may seem that meanings are being directly exchanged via the words and gestures being used. But they are not. Each speaker is using the signals of the other to construct, test and anticipate the meaning they believe the other intends. You can observe this happening by noticing the many check questions that we use during our conversations. For example we may interrupt things with *"Just a second, what did you mean by …?"* or *"So what you seem to be saying is …"* or *"I can see where you're coming from/going with this, but …".*

Fluent speakers of a common natural language are able to exchange words, actions and gestures etc as if these signals were meaning itself. But in reality, it is

the familiarity of the signals, and shared values within a common culture in which they are embedded, that enables a receiver to construct meaning. For the most part, the meaning constructed is consistent with what the speaker intended – but not always, as we shall see shortly.

All this leads us nicely to a definition of communication.

*Human communication is the process of influencing a human receiver to create thought and action that is consistent with, and responsive to, the sender's purpose.*

A common language, context and culture always increases the speed and bandwidth by which intended communications can occur. However, these commonalities do not eliminate the construction of unintended meanings. Many communication failures arise precisely because people fail to recognise that they are exchanging signals that have as many possible meanings as can be constructed by the receiver, and not just the single meaning intended by the sender.

If the communication takes place between team members, then any command or response always takes place in the context of the team's greater purpose. This means that effective communication in a team requires every team member to understand not only their own communication needs, but also how these dovetail with the communication needs of other team members.

> It's not enough to transmit a signal. It's about facilitating its interpretation, too.

The story of what happened on the bridge of *Pride of Provence* on a spring afternoon in 2003 illustrates something of the difference between successful signal transmission on the one hand, and successful human communication on the other.

## Case study: Dented *Pride*[1]

At precisely 17.13 on a pleasant afternoon in April 2003, the 641 passengers and crew onboard the cross channel ro-ro P&O passenger ferry *Pride of Provence* reached Point Alpha on the approach to Dover. Point Alpha is 3 miles from port – the designated reporting range. The Chief Officer was at the con and, exactly as required, he radioed the ferry's approach to Dover Port Control.

The crossing had been uneventful. It was still daylight, the weather was good and the visibility clear. The ferry was heading west, aiming for the gap between the two breakwater arms that marked the entrance to Dover harbour and the ro-ro berths inside. The bridge team was aware that a strong north-easterly wind would be blowing from the ferry's starboard quarter as she sailed through the gap, and that a southerly tidal stream was flowing across the harbour entrance.

Port Control gave the Chief Officer permission for *Pride of Provence* to close to one mile, and at 17.18, when the ferry was two miles out, the Master took the con and began to reduce her 19.5 knots cruising speed. At 17.19, Port Control informed

the ferry that a Sea France ferry, *Cezanne*, was swinging inside the harbour walls in preparation for reversing into her berth. *Pride's* Master confirmed to Port Control that he would wait for *Cezanne*, but would continue to close.

**Communications were poor – despite lots of relevant messages.**

At 17.20, the bridge team (Chief Officer, a Second Officer, a cadet, the helmsman and a lookout) listened as the *Pride's* Master briefed them on his plan. Also present was a supernumerary Master who was there to observe the manoeuvre. *Pride's* Master outlined his intention to go through the middle of the breakwater ends, not getting closer than 30 yards to either one. Once inside, they would run up the inside of the eastern breakwater before entering No 2 berth.

Everybody was in their proper position as the ferry slowed further and, at a half a mile out, the stabiliser fins were taken in by the Chief Officer, as the Master had instructed. In line with normal practice, the Master was giving orders to the helmsman in the form of landmarks to steer towards. Just after his briefing, the Master ordered the helmsman to steer towards the middle of the entrance and then, a bit later, towards the end of the southern breakwater. Inside the breakwaters, *Cezanne* was still manoeuvring. Port Control called *Pride's* Master to confirm his intentions. The Master re-confirmed his plan to come through the gap, run down the breakwater arm and then on to the

berth. Port Control reminded *Pride's* Master that *Cezanne* had only just begun to go astern into her berth.

At 17.23, as *Pride of Provence* neared the harbour entrance, her Master started a swing to starboard. At 17.24, the end of the southern breakwater was 150 yards on the port side of the bridge and the ferry was swinging sharply. Frustrated by the slow progress of *Cezanne*, the Master ordered *Pride's* helmsman to steer further to starboard. 15 seconds later he increased the speed and the turn still further. With his eye on the end of the southern breakwater, the port lookout had been calling "running clear", but now he suddenly called "starting to close a bit", then "closing in on the end". The Master realised the ferry was turning before it had got through the gap. He ordered hard to port, but it was too late. With the ferry still swinging rapidly to starboard, the port side of the stern made heavy contact with the end of the southern breakwater.

Passengers and crew were thrown to the deck, tables and chairs were overturned, and the shelves in the shopping areas violently ejected their stock over the floor. Thirty people were later treated for their injuries which included broken bones and lacerations as people collided with unyielding surfaces. Nine were hospitalised, but later released. The contact with the breakwater caused substantial structural damage to the stern from decks 2 to 8, but the ferry made it to berth an hour later with the assistance of tugs. On the vehicle deck, cargoes had shifted within trucks and they needed to be re-stowed once ashore. As it turned

**With no shared plan, they couldn't help each other.**

out, had the contact with the breakwater not been made, it was highly likely that a close-quarters situation would have occurred between *Pride of Provence* and *Cezanne.*

The accident report concluded that the most important failing was poor communication. But how was it that despite a constant stream of relevant messages throughout the incident, something was missed? And what was it?

The answer lies in the Master's briefing. Although he declared his intention for the approach to the Dover berth, and he assigned suitably experienced staff to monitor progress, he did not explain the plan for achieving his intention. As a result, the bridge team had nothing to monitor their progress against. If the ferry's approach from two miles out had been agreed and steady, then the track could have been monitored using radar parallel indexing, target trails, or shore-based landmarks. In this way, the agreed approach could have been maintained for speed and direction against the varying strengths of tidal stream and wind.

Similarly, when the lookout was monitoring the ferry's position relative to the breakwater on the ship's port side, he could only do so moment-by-moment rather than against an agreed course change plan. As a result, the possibility for anticipating future problems was severely reduced and the sudden closing of the ferry on the breakwater was as much a surprise for the lookout as it was for the Master. The lookout was not aware of the Master's second-by-second course and speed adjustments, and the Master's location on the central bridge con meant he was unable to appreciate the vessel's

position or rate of swing relative to the breakwater. The whole bridge team was living 'in the moment' and had lost a key component of situation awareness – the ability to mentally project themselves into the immediate future (see section on *Making decisions*). They could react, but with no shared plan, they couldn't anticipate.

The relevant parties were passing relevant messages, but they weren't sharing the same overall understanding. Without a common understanding, they were not so much a team as an audience for the Master as he found himself orchestrating a multi-person manoeuvre single-handed.

## What does communication require?

The denting of the *Pride of Provence* shows that even when there are lots of signals being passed, communication can still fail. So what are the requirements for successful human communication? There are two:

- People must have different perspectives

- They must have a shared means to explore the differences

### Different perspectives

Both parties experience the world differently, but with enough similarity to be able to explore the differences. If their experience was identical in every respect, no

communication would be needed. At the other extreme, if there were no similarities, there could be no common starting point to explore their differences.

### Common dialogue

We all have different points of view. For communication to be successful, we must have the means to realise that we do – and understand the differences between them. We can achieve this through a common dialogue in which we ask questions, provide answers, give commands, make responses and demonstrate agreements.

> Dialogue is not the same as speaking a language.

Dialogue is not the same as speaking to one another in a language like English, Russian or Tagalog. Languages provide rich possibilities for dialogue, but we can achieve dialogue in many other ways, eg through sign language, gesture, codes, computer graphical user interfaces, radio protocols, and the jargon, body language and informal shorthand gestures that (for example) crew members invent for themselves.

We all share basic biological similarities that enable us to communicate even though we may have completely different cultures and languages. For example, everyone – whether they are English, Russian or Filipino – understands hunger, thirst, fatigue and temperature extremes. If they were all put together in the same environment, they would easily find a way of communicating their needs about these things to each other – even without a common language. However, their ability to communicate with each other over more technical collaborations – like navigating, or crewing a ship – would be more of a challenge.

At the other end of the scale, even with a common language plus full training and lots of experience, their different cultures and associated value systems would interfere with communications (see panel, *How do you do?*).

But even when we share the same language, culture, country, town and street, successful communication cannot be guaranteed. This is because we are still responsible for creating our own understanding based on our individual ambitions, needs and experiences (see section, *Making sense of things*). We don't simply receive signals: we search within ourselves for what the signals mean. Furthermore, the meaning we find is only ever understandable in terms of the concepts and values we already have.

This means that to communicate effectively, we need to spend as much effort successfully empathising with each other as deciding what we want to communicate. Mentally putting ourselves in the place of the receiver helps us to construct the message we want to convey so that it will have the intended impact. It follows that the more training and mutual experience we have, the more accurate the empathy, and the more efficient and



effective the communication will be (see panel, *Stirred, but not shaken*).

## How much of a problem is communication failure?

It is very serious. Communication failures happen frequently and have serious consequences in safety-critical industries. For example:

- In the UK rail industry, communication failures are the main feature in 25% of accidents[2]. For accidents involving track workers, this proportion rises to 50%.

- In the Australian aviation industry, communication failures account for 20% of accidents[3].

- In the US general aviation industry (smaller, private aircraft), 30% of incidents are caused by miscommunications[4].

- In the defence sector, major disasters have been caused by multiple communication failures both within teams and between flight crews and ground controllers. These include the shooting down of a Libyan airliner by the Israeli Defence Forces in 1973, the shooting down of an Iranian Airbus by the USS *Vincennes* in 1988, and the shooting down of two Black Hawk helicopters carrying UN VIPs by the US Air Force in 1994. Communication failures are also a major component of most military fratricide (friendly fire) incidents.

- In the US health sector, communications errors have been found to be the cause of in-hospital deaths twice as frequently as inadequate clinical skills[5]. Other US studies have revealed that communication failures account for up to 60% of all errors recorded in operating rooms and intensive care units[6].

# At least 25% of accidents involve communications failures.

## Why does human communication fail?

As we have seen, people need to have different points of view in order for communication to be required at all. This requirement is easy to meet since it is in an inevitable part of being human that people form their own individual views from the information available to them. However, these differences in perspective are also the source of misunderstandings if dialogue is interrupted – or omitted – before shared meaning can be established.

The level of training and experience on *Pride of Provence* meant that the bridge team understood their instructions and the technical aspects of the harbour approach.

However, they didn't notice that they had not given each other the necessary means to carry out their monitoring functions. Or if they did notice, they did not know how to intervene in order to correct things.

What happened on *Pride of the Provence* neatly illustrates the two main reasons why human communications fail:

- **Insufficient dialogue** – where an important difference between people's understanding remains undetected

- **Insufficient opportunity for dialogue** – where a difference is suspected, or detected, but is not resolved in time

## How can communication failures be prevented?

How do these dialogue insufficiencies arise? And how can they be addressed? Here are six ways. All need to be overcome in order to ensure that people are able to engage in the dialogue necessary to live in a world of shared meaning.

- **Lack of media skills and knowledge** People may know what needs to be communicated, when, and to whom, but are physically unable to do so. This may be due to operations in a noisy environment, lack of training in the use of the communications equipment, or the failure to share (enough of) a common language[7]. These factors are best addressed by appropriate recruitment and selection policies, procedural training courses, and procedure-based manuals. Training in Standard Marine Communication Phrases (SMCP) is an essential foundation for ensuring clearer safety-related verbal communication at sea.

# Preventing communication failures requires action at all organisational levels.


[2] Based on an analysis of 391 accident reports, Shanahan et al (2006)
[3] Based on an analysis of 175 accident reports, McMillan (1998)
[4] Based on an analysis of 200 incident reports, Etem & Patten (1998)
[5] Based on an analysis of 16,000 hospital deaths, Parker & Coiera (2000)
[6] Weinger & Blike (2003)

[7] The ISM Code and STCW 95 both mandate the use of a common language, but do not specify proficiency levels, despite the existence of the internationally recognised IELTS (International English Language Testing System), which has been adapted for seafarers.

- **Lack of task skills and knowledge** People may not have enough training or experience in their own job to know what information it is important to communicate and when. This is best addressed by task training to defined performance standards, with appropriate refresher training to prevent skill fade (see section on *Learning and development*). Particularly important in the maritime industry is the provision of well-designed, properly translated shipboard documentation and procedure-based manuals that can be understood by their target audience.

- **Lack of team task skills and knowledge** People may not understand enough about the information requirements of their fellow team members – or the overall team task – to anticipate what is useful (or critical) for others to know, or when they need to know it. This is best addressed by team training, eg Bridge Resource Management, tabletop exercises, team briefings, seminar discussions, and lectures (see section on *Working with others*).

- **Lack of social skills or cultural knowledge** People may not possess the personal skills needed to engage effectively with other people. This includes knowing how to overcome personal differences or incompatibilities so that they do not interfere with effective performance. It also includes knowing how to get the best out of people, motivating them and encouraging them to work with each other (see section on *Working with others*). Or people may not appreciate how cultural differences affect people's understanding of different communication styles. This is best addressed by personal skills, leadership, cultural awareness and diversity and equality training programmes.

- **Lack of communications process skills and knowledge** People may not understand enough about their own – and others – mental processes involved in successful communication. As a result, they may not be sufficiently disciplined in their assessment of the information quality they receive, or in the inferences and associated risks they take before using it. This is best addressed by training in leadership and critical thinking[8].

- **Lack of time** People may be surprised by fast-moving, sudden or emergency conditions. Lack of time can also arise through high workload, leading to slips and lapses: people can simply forget to communicate or be distracted by having too much to do. This is best addressed by good job design, mentoring, task and team training programmes across a wide range of scenarios, and regular team-based emergency drills.

## Around the buoys again

The main points covered by this section are as follows:

To an engineer, information transfer involves transmitters, receivers and signal-to-noise ratios. Human communication is much more complicated because meaning is not directly transferred. Instead, people create meaning for themselves based on what they already know and expect, and are able to attend to. Human communication is the process of influencing a human receiver to create thought and action that is consistent with, and responsive to, the sender's purpose.

---

[8] For example, Fisher et al (1997)

DO ensure that communication training in your organisation pays attention to the full range of skills and knowledge that underpin successful communication – including common language and protocols, individual task competence, team roles and objectives, leadership, personal skills, cultural awareness and critical thinking.

DO encourage staff to ask – and answer – clarifying questions. Many communication failures happen because people, or their colleagues, are in different situations to the ones they think they are in.

DO be aware of the greatly increased risk of communication failure when people have a heavy workload. The distraction of too many things to do in too little time is a frequent cause of forgotten or incomplete communications. If people are busy, you may need to work differently to get the information you need.

DO be aware of the greatly increased risk of communication failure with people who lack experience. They may not look for a vital piece of information, detect it, or recognise its importance. They may not know how to communicate it, who to tell, when to do so, how to tell it has been understood, or what to do if it hasn't.

In the process of human communication, the sender and receiver need to connect with each other via a suitable dialogue that allows the necessary questions, answers, commands and responses to take place, and the resulting agreements to be made, together with whatever evidence might be required to substantiate them.

Dialogue is not the same as speaking a language. Languages provide rich possibilities for dialogue, but dialogue can be achieved in many other ways, eg through sign language, gesture, codes, computer graphical user interfaces, radio protocols and shorthand jargon that people invent for themselves.

Human communication fails because people do not engage in dialogue that will result in unambiguous agreement about the situation they share and the possibilities that are open to them. There are several reasons for inadequate dialogue:

- People may have inadequate access to common media for the dialogue (eg no common language)

- People may have inadequate technical training (eg unawareness that communication is necessary)

- People may have inadequate personal skills or cultural awareness training (eg unawareness that information content or communication style may be interpreted differently in different cultures)

- People may have inadequate critical abilities (eg lack of appreciation of the discipline that successful communication requires)

Communication failures are common and have serious consequences in safety-critical industries like seafaring. These failures have been shown to account for in excess of 25% of accidents in a range of such industries. Each of the sources of inadequate dialogue must be addressed at all appropriate organisational levels if communication failures are to be avoided.

## Deeper waters

This section has drawn on these books and papers:


ALERT! (2007) *Effective Communication*, The International Maritime Human Element Bulletin Issue No. 14 May 2007. Nautical Institute, sponsored by Lloyds Register

Etem K. & Patten M. (1998) *Communications-related incidents in General Aviation dual flight training*. ASRS Directline, Issue No. 10, December 1998

Fisher A. & Scrive, M. (1997). *Critical thinking: Its definition and assessment*. Centre for Research in Critical Thinking. Norwich/Edgepress, California, USA

Hofstede G. (1994) *Cultures and Organizations: intercultural cooperation and its importance for survival*, HarperCollinsBusiness

MAIB (2003b) *Report on the investigation of the contact between Pride of Provence and The Southern Breakwater, Dover Harbour, eastern entrance on 18 April 2003*, Marine Accident Investigation Branch, Southampton, UK, Report No 26/2003, Nov 2003

McMillan D. (1998) *"…Say again…?" Miscommunications in Air Traffic Control*, Thesis, Queensland Univ of Tech

Parker J. & Coiera E. (2000) *Improving clinical communication: A view from Psychology*, Journal of the American Medical Informatics Association, Vol. 7, No. 5, Sep/Oct 2000

Pask G. (1976) *Conversation Theory: Applications in Education and Epistemology*, Elsevier

Shanahan P., Gregory D., Nicol A. & Fulthorpe B. (2006) *The role of communication errors in incident causation*, Rail Safety and Standards Board, London, Project T365

Weinger M.B. & Blike G.T. (2003) *Intubation mishap*, http://webmm.ahrq.gov/case.aspx?caseID=29 (Mar '10)

# Taking the con

## Working with human behaviour

This Guide has explored eight fundamental aspects of normal human behaviour. Each section has looked at how their characteristics continuously influence what we think and do as we go about our daily activities.

They are what they are. And they are what makes us human. Whether you consider yourself as an individual or as part of a large corporation, these characteristics influence your ideas, your ambitions, and your strength to achieve them. In a safety-critical enterprise such as the shipping industry, they also carry with them the potential for catastrophic failure, devastating loss, large-scale destruction of lives and livelihoods, financial ruin and business collapse.

As said before in this Guide, we are all the secret of our successes and the victims of our failures.

The characteristics of human behaviour depicted in this Guide will not go away and cannot be ignored. Understanding and working with them is not just an essential duty of the organisations that make up the shipping industry. It is what gives a sustainable and competitive edge to the companies who are most successful at it.

## So, how do you do it?

In exploring each of the aspects of human behaviour, a number of past maritime accidents have been re-analysed in this Guide. The aim has been to bring a clearer understanding of human behaviour at work. Hopefully, these accounts will serve as a foundation for thinking about other accidents, near-misses and 'what-ifs' in your own experience – as well as the normal, every day practice around you.

Each section has ended with a series of DOs and DON'Ts that summarise best practice in each area. Organisations would do well to examine each of these carefully with a view to addressing what they mean to them in their own operational context. The following questions may be useful in this regard.

### Making the DOs happen

- Do we already do this (or are we planning to do it)?

- If so, is it part of a strategic initiative that has the full support of our top management? Should it be?

- If this is not being addressed, why not?

- What – and who – will it take to get it started?

- What could it cost us if we ignore this?

### Stopping the DON'Ts from happening

- Do we know if we are doing this and how much? How can we find out?

- What will we need to do and how will we need to change to stop it happening?

- What could it cost us if we do not address this?

## The view from the wheelhouse

Perhaps the most important organisational insight that we would like to leave you with is the same one that Sophie tried to capture in the diagram she used to escape the devil and the deep blue sea at the beginning of this book.

It is this. Everything in an enterprise such as shipping is connected to everything else. The industry operates as a single, complex system, and activity in any one part will, sooner or later, create a response somewhere else. Sometimes, if we ask the right questions, it is possible to foresee where this response might be. Such questions allow us to see that if we focus on doing what seems to be best in a small area without regard for its wider impact, we may harm the overall system.

A good example of this is the attempt to optimise safety through exponentially increasing rules and laws. While this makes standards explicit, it can also lead (for example) to increasing criminalisation of Masters, which can lead to increasing numbers leaving for shore jobs as soon as they are qualified. This in turn can lead to accelerated seafarer promotion, which can result in a decrease in expertise in highly responsible jobs that keep getting more complex – and the continuation of an accident rate that won't go down.

Quite often, it is not possible to predict exactly how the system will respond to optimisations of local problems, but there is great benefit in anticipating that there will be some sort of response – and looking for it actively. Failure to do this simply makes us victims of the law of unintended consequences.

The global shipping industry is a complex system activated by human behaviour. But it is also important to understand that the eight aspects of human behaviour described in this Guide are all smaller parts of a single system.

Almost every moment of our waking lives involves us in making sense of things, taking a risk, making a decision, learning, communicating as we work with each other, getting tired as we do it and, sometimes, making a mistake. We do these things not only every day, but often simultaneously, and they interact with each other.

Just as for the overall shipping system, it follows that attempts to improve particular aspects of human behaviour may not be the best for achieving what organisations require from human behaviour as a whole.

For example:

- Organisational initiatives designed to increase safe behaviour will not fare well unless operational efficiency practices and targets are also overhauled.

- Fatigue management programmes will not work in the absence of boardroom decisions about complementary manning policies or without ship designers who can distinguish between health and safety.



- Companies will remain ignorant about the true level of expertise in their organisations unless they invest in training and its proper evaluation, and are able to coordinate with ship and equipment designers so that training can be delivered at the point and time of need.

- Excessive risk-taking and complacency among staff cannot be addressed without attention being paid to the organisational role in the reasons why people ignore or break rules.

- Organisations cannot effectively address improvements to their safety culture, or reduce the costs of the accidents they suffer, without replacing blame attribution by accountability within a 'just culture'.

- Companies cannot improve on the cost and waste of communication failures without investing in effective teamwork training.

- The effectiveness of training cannot be improved without realising that instructors need teaching skills as much as they need to be subject matter experts.

All of these examples are the result of *systems thinking*. This is concerned with identifying the components of a whole system, and examining them in terms of their influence on each other.

In the first section of this Guide (*Between the devil and the deep blue sea*), Sophie's world provided a good illustration of an influence diagram based on systems thinking.

---

### What is resilience engineering?

Resilience engineering is concerned with systems that are able to sustain operations in the face of disturbances that are both expected and unexpected. Resilience engineering starts by recognising that complex, tightly interconnected systems (like the shipping industry) generate a wide range of behaviour (including human behaviour) that will never be completely predictable.

It further recognises that rules and procedures will therefore never be complete and that the real value of human operators is that they can continually adjust to compensate. However, because of incomplete information, approximations and time constraints, this also means that occasionally the system will produce failure.

In resilience engineering, failures are characterised not as adverse events that are caused by human error, or which slip between the cracks of a Safety Management System (SMS). Instead, they are conceived as small variations in normal system performance that combine to produce dangerous levels of resonance – much as soldiers marching in step over a bridge can destroy it. When components are tightly interconnected, resonance is magnified and travels quickly between apparently remote components.

Resilience engineering is now producing tools (eg FRAM, Functional Resonance Assessment Method) aimed at predicting where resonance may occur and how to develop effective countermeasures.

*For further information, see Hollnagel (2006) and Eurocontrol (2009)*

---

While systems thinking has been widely explored for 30 years or so[1], its recent application in resilience engineering is of particular relevance to the shipping industry (see panel, *What is resilience engineering?*).

The diagram opposite gives the wheelhouse view of what we have been concerned with in this Guide.

---

[1] For example, Checkland (1981), Churchman (1984), Senge (1990).

**Everyone's view is different.** When we forget this, our assumptions become dangerous.
**What we see** is affected by what we need, our self-image, what we have done in the past, and what we want from the future.
**Training and experience** make it easier for us to share the same assumptions - but it's not guaranteed, and we can never share the same view.

**Human communication** is not just about transmitting a signal. It's about doing so in a way that facilitates an appropriate response to its intended interpretation.
**Communication fails** when not enough is specified by either party to assure intended interpretation. This may be due to bad assumptions about each other's context, or insufficient opportunity to check those assumptions.
**Communication failures** cause 25% of safety-critical accidents and significant, avoidable expense every year.

**Risk perception** is affected by how much control we think we have, and how familiar and valuable something is for us.
**Risk cannot be eliminated** because our world is uncertain.
**We need to take risks** to keep things interesting. If things become boring or uneventful, we take more risks.
**Risk-taking becomes dangerous** when the gap between actual probability and our perception of it becomes too great. This results in a wide range of human behaviour from complacency, through bad decisions to catastrophic action.

**As individuals,** we work with others to assess them, confront difficult issues and negotiate with them. Each of these areas requires re-usable skills and best practice that everyone can acquire. Doing so makes us more productive.
**As team members,** working with others requires a further set of skills that must also be learned if organisations wish to maximise the efficiency of their operating schedules and avoid undue expense.

**We make decisions** based on our past experience and we tend to follow the course of least resistance. This is determined by a trade-off between the thoroughness demanded of us and the time and resources available to us.
**Expert decision-making** takes at least 10 years to acquire.
**People and organisations** favour efficiency over thoroughness because it's cheaper and quicker. Rules created to increase our thoroughness can get broken if we see a more efficient way of getting the job done.

**We learn** all the time - we can't help it.
**Learning requires activity by the learner.** Teachers do not transmit knowledge - they can only facilitate its acquisition.
**Organisations need to take control of what people learn.** Failing to do so leaves people to learn from each other, possibly resulting in the acquisition of bad practice and dangerously incomplete knowledge.
**Investment in training** increases productivity, reduces staffing problems and helps create a 'just culture'

**Making mistakes** is normal. Mistakes are influenced by individual factors like fatigue and stress and by organisational factors like job design and deadlines.
**Hindsight is the illusion** that mistakes can be eliminated. Mistakes are simply the name we give to normal system behaviour that we don't want.
**The pursuit of a 'just culture'** is the best approach to developing a safety culture that stops mistakes becoming disasters by influencing all organisational levels.

**Fatigue is a normal human response to a normal situation.** Sleep is the only fix - nothing else will do.
**Fatigue becomes dangerous** when deep or dream sleep is denied. Being awake 24 hours degrades our performance the same as being 25% over the UK drink-drive limit.
**Fatigue is effectively dealt with** via a fatigue management plan operated at all organisational levels from boardroom to ship's crew.
**Stress is a normal human response to a bad situation.** It is dangerous to both people and company operations. It must be designed against, listened for, and managed away.

The diagram depicts the key components that each shipping organisation should aim to integrate into its own systems model of operation. In doing so, each organisation will define for itself the extent and nature of the cooperative relationships it needs with others.

One thing is sure. It is only when each shipping organisation models itself as part of a single global system and starts using the tools that resilience engineering is beginning to provide that the most powerful answers will start to emerge to the question of how to deal most effectively with the human element.

On page 5 of this Guide, Pogo expresses the viewpoint that: *"We have met the enemy, and he is us"*. While amusing, we hope you agree that this view is both fatalistic and unhelpful. To the contrary, it is the point of this Guide that: *"We have seen the answer, and it is us"*.

**Deeper waters**

Checkland P. (1981) *Systems Thinking, Systems Practice*. (Wiley)

Churchman C.W. (1984 - revised) *The Systems Approach*. (Delacorte Press)

Eurocontrol (2009) *A White Paper on Resilience Engineering for Air Traffic Management*, European Organisation for the safety of Air Navigation (Eurocontrol)

Hollnagel E., Woods D.D. & Leveson N. (2006) *Resilience engineering: Concepts and precepts*. Aldershot, UK: Ashgate

Senge P.M. (1990) *The Fifth Discipline – The Art & Practice of The Learning Organization*. (Currency Doubleday)

# Bibliography


ABS (2001) *Crew Habitability on Ships, American Bureau of Shipping*, Dec 2001

ALERT! (2007) *Time to wake up to the consequences of fatigue*, The International Maritime Human Element Bulletin, The Nautical Institute, Issue No. 13 January 2007

Anderson J.R. (1982) *Acquisition of cognitive skill*. Psychological Review, 89, 369-406

Australian Government (2000) *Beyond the Midnight Oil: An Inquiry into Managing Fatigue in Transport*, House of Representatives Transport Committee, Australian Government

Bailey N. (2007) *Marine Incidents: Ways of Seeing, SIRC Symposium 2007*, Seafarers International Research Centre, Cardiff University

Bailey N., Ellis N. & Sampson H. (2006) *Perceptions of Risk in the Maritime Industry*, Seafarers International Research Institute (SIRC)

Calhoun S.R. (LT) & Lamb T. (1999) *Human Factors in Ship Design: Preventing and Reducing Shipboard Operator Fatigue*, University of Michigan Department of Naval Architecture and Marine Engineering U.S. Coast Guard Research Project

Checkland P. (1981) *Systems Thinking, Systems Practice*, Wiley

Churchman C.W. (1984 - revised) *The Systems Approach*. Delacorte Press

Cialdini R.B. (2009) *Influence: Science and practice*, Pearson International Edition, Fifth Edition

Cranfield School of Management (2008) *Impact of Investors in People on People Management Practices and Firm Performance*

Dekker S.W.A. (2007) *Just Culture: Balancing safety and Accountability*, Ashgate Publishing Ltd

Earthy J.V. & Sherwood Jones B.M. (2006) *Design for the human factor: the move to goal-based rules*, Lloyds Register

Ellis N., Sampson H., Aguado J.C., Baylon A., Del Rosario L., Lim Y.F. & Veiga, J. (2005) *What Seafarers think of CBT*, Seafarers International Research Centre (SIRC) Cardiff University http://www.sirc.cf.ac.uk/pdf/CBT%20Report.pdf (in Mar '10)

Endsley M. (1999) *Situation Awareness In Aviation Systems*, in Garland D.J., Wise J.A. & Hopkin V.D. (Eds), Handbook of Aviation Human Factors, Mahwah, NJ: Lawrence Erlbaum Associates

Energy Institute (2009) *Hearts and Minds Programme*, http://www.eimicrosites.org/heartsandminds/index.php (in Mar '10)

Ericsson K.A. (2006) *The Cambridge Handbook of Expertise and Expert Performance*, Cambridge University Press

Etem K. & Patten M. (1998) *Communications-related incidents in General Aviation dual flight training*. ASRS Directline, Issue No. 10, December 1998

Eurocontrol (1999) Human Factors Module A Business Case for Human Factors Investment Report No. HUM. ET1.ST13.4000-REP-02

Eurocontrol (2009) *A White Paper on Resilience Engineering for Air Traffic Management*, European Organisation for the safety of Air Navigation Eurocontrol

Fisher A. & Scriven M. (1997). *Critical thinking: Its definition and assessment*. Centre for Research in Critical Thinking. Norwich/Edgepress, California, USA

Fisher R., Ury W. & Patton B. (1992) *Getting to Yes*, 2nd Edition, Random House Business Books

Flin R., O'Connor P. & Crichton, M. (2008) *Safety at the Sharp End: A Guide to Non-Technical Skills*, Ashgate Publishing Ltd

Gagné R.M. Briggs L.J. & Wager W.W. (1992) *Principles of Instructional Design*, Holt, Rinehart & Winston

GAIN Working Group E (2004) *A Roadmap to a Just Culture: Enhancing the Safety Environment*, First Edition, Sep 2004, Flight Ops/ATC Ops Safety Info. Sharing

Gregory Harland Ltd (1999) *Development of a skill fade model*, GHL/CHS/SkillFade/Deliverables/FinalReport/ Volume1/v3.0, Centre for Human Sciences, DERA

Hofstede G. (1994) *Cultures and Organizations: intercultural cooperation and its importance for survival*, HarperCollinsBusiness

Hollnagel E. (2009) *The ETTO Principle: Efficiency - Thoroughness Trade-Off: Why Things That Go Right Sometimes Go Wrong*, Ashgate Publishing Ltd

Hollnagel E., Woods D.D. & Leveson N. (2006) *Resilience engineering: Concepts and precepts*. Aldershot, UK: Ashgate Publishing Ltd

HSE (2004) *Work-related stress: a short guide*, Health & Safety Executive

HSE (2006) *Fatigue and Risk Index*: In Nov 2009, the report is at http://www.hse.gov.uk/research/rrpdf/rr446.pdf (in Mar '10)

Hudson P.T.W. (2007) *What is the Hearts and Minds Programme?* Powerpoint presentation at http://www. riskinsite.com.au/sicorp_web/Events/07OHSSeminar/ Day%201/Patrick%20Hudson.ppt (in Sep 09)

Hudson P.T.W. & Parker D. (2002) *Profiling safety culture: The OGP interview study*. Report to OGP. London. Leiden University, Department of Psychology
Investors In People (IIP)
http://www.investorsinpeople.co.uk (in Mar '10)

Klein G. (1999) *Sources of power: How people make decisions*, The MIT Press

Lewis R.D. (2006) *When Cultures Collide*, Nicholas Brealey Publishing

Lloyd's Register (2000) *World Casualty Statistics*. London: Lloyd's Register: http://www.lrfairplay.com/Maritime_ data/statistics.html (in Mar '10)

LUL (2007) *Integration of Human Factors into Systems Development*, London Underground Ltd, Standard 1-217 v. A1, Oct 2007, LUL/WN/00834

Lützhöft M.H. and Dekker S.W.A. (2002) *On Your Watch: Automation on the Bridge*. Journal of Navigation, 55(1), 83-96

MAIB (1999) *Investigation into the collision between the UK registered cargo vessel Hoo Robin and the Republic of Ireland registered cargo vessel Arklow Marsh on the River Trent on 2 March 1999*, Marine Accident Investigation Branch, Carlton House, Carlton Place, Southampton, SO15 2DZ, File 1/3/66

MAIB (2003a) *Report on the investigation on the collision between mv Ash and mv Dutch Aquamarine in the SW lane of the Dover Strait TSS with the loss of one life, 9 October 2001*, Marine Accident Investigation Branch, First Floor, Carlton House, Carlton Place, Southampton, UK, SO15 2DZ, Report No 7/2003, March 2003

MAIB (2003b) *Report on the investigation of the contact between Pride of Provence and The Southern Breakwater, Dover Harbour, eastern entrance on 18 April 2003*, Marine Accident Investigation Branch, Southampton, UK, Report No 26/2003, Nov 2003

MAIB (2008) *Part 1 - Merchant Vessels, Case 7: Main Boiler Chemical Clean Ends in Fatal Explosion*, Safety Digest 2/2008, http://www.maib.gov.uk/publications/safety_ digests/2008/safetydigest_2_2008.cfm (in Mar '10)

MAIB (2009a) *Investigation Report on the Saga Rose (synopsis), Report No. 1/2009, 6 Jan 2009*; http://www. maib.gov.uk/publications/investigation_reports/2009/ saga_rose.cfm (in Mar '10)

MAIB (2009b) *Report on the investigation of the grounding of Antari near Larne, Northern Ireland, 29 Jun 2008*, Marine Accident Investigation Branch, First Floor, Carlton House, Carlton Place, Southampton, UK, SO15 2DZ, Report No 7/2009, Feb 2009

Maslow A. (1943) *A Theory of Human Motivation*, Psychological Review, 50, 370-396

Maturana H.M. & Varela F.J. (1980) *Autopoeisis and Cognition: The Realization of the Living*, Dordrecht: D. Reidel Vol 42 Boston Studies in the Philosophy of Science

MCA, *Leading for Safety: a practical guide for leaders in the Maritime Industry*, Maritime and Coastguard Agency, MCA 140

McMillan D. (1998) *"…Say again…?" Miscommunications in Air Traffic Control*, Thesis, Queensland University of Technology

Milgram S. (1974) *Obedience to authority: An experimental view*. Harper & Row

MOD (2008) *DefStan 00-250 Human Factors for Designers of Systems, Pts 0 - 4*, UK Ministry of Defence Internet http://www.dstan.mod.uk (in Mar '10)

Moore-Ede M., Heitmann A., Dawson T. & Guttkuhn R. (2005) *Truckload Driver Accident, Injury and Turnover Rates Reduced by Fatigue Risk-Informed Performance-Based Safety Program*. Transport Canada: Proceedings of the 2005 International Conference on Fatigue Management in Transportation Operations, September 2005, Seattle. http://www.tc.gc.ca/innovation/tdc/publication/ tp14620/h04.htm (in Mar '10)

Morel G., Amalberti R. & Chuavin C. (2008) *Articulating the differences between safety and resilience: the decision making process of professional sea-fishing skippers*, Human Factors Vol 50, No. 1, February 2008 pp 1-16

Murphy P.J. (2002) *Fatigue management during Operations: A Commander's Guide*, Defence Science and Technology Organisation, Australian Department of Defence (Army)

NTSB (2009) *Allision of Hong Kong, Registered Containership M/V Cosco Busan with the Delta Tower of the San Francisco–Oakland Bay Bridge San Francisco, California, November 7, 2007*, National Transportation Safety Board, NTSB/MAR-09/01, PB2009-916401

Parker A.W., Hubinger L.M., Green S., Sargaent L. & Boyd R. (1997) *A Survey of the Health, Stress and Fatigue of Australian Seafarers*. Canberra: Australian Maritime Safety Authority

Parker J. & Coiera E. (2000) *Improving clinical communication: A view from Psychology*, Journal of the American Medical Informatics Association, Vol. 7, No. 5, Sep/Oct 2000

Pask G. (1976) *Conversation Theory*, Applications in Education and Epistemology, Elsevier

Piattelli-Palmarini M. (1994) *Inevitable illusions: how mistakes of reason rule our minds*, John Wiley & Sons Inc Rasmussen J. (1979): *On the Structure of Knowledge – a Morphology of Mental Models in a Man-Machine System Context*. Risø-M-2192, 1979

Reason J. (1990) *Human Error*. New York: Cambridge University Press

Reason J. (1997) *Managing the risks of organisational accidents*, Hants, England, Ashgate Publishing Ltd

RSSB (2004) *Teamworking in the railway industry: The Journey Guide*. Toolset produced for the Rail Safety and Standards Board by Gregory Harland Ltd http://www.rssb.co.uk/pdf/reports/research/ Teamworking%20in%20the%20railway%20industry%20 -%20The%20Journey%20Guide.pdf (in Mar '10)

RSSB (2006) *Coping with Shift Work & Fatigue: a good practice guide for drivers*, Rail Safety and Standards Board, London

RSSB (2008) *Understanding Human Factors – a guide for the railway industry*, Rail Safety and Standards Board, Angel Square, 1 Torrens Street, London EC1V 1NY. http://www.rssb.co.uk/expertise/human_factors/human_factors_good_practices_guide.asp (in Mar '10)

Salas E., Sims D.E. & Burke C.S. (2005) *Is there a big five in teamwork?* Small Group Research, 36, 155

Salas E., Cooke N.J. & Rosen M.A. (2008) *On teams, teamwork and team performance: Discoveries and developments*. Human Factors, 50, 3, pp. 540-547

Senge P.M. (1990) *The Fifth Discipline – The Art & Practice of The Learning Organization,* Currency Doubleday

Shanahan P., Gregory D., Nicol A. & Fulthorpe B. (2006) *The role of communication errors in incident causation*, Rail Safety and Standards Board, London, Project T365

Shell (2006) *The Shell Sustainability Report 2006*, http://sustainabilityreport.shell.com/2006/responsibleenergy/personalandprocesssafety/changingbehaviour.html (in Mar '10)

Slovic P. (2000) *The perception of risk*, Earthscan Publications Ltd

Smith A., Allen P. & Wadsworth E. (2006) *Seafarer Fatigue: The Cardiff Research Programme*, Centre for Occupational & Health Psychology, Cardiff University

Sprent P. (1988) *Taking risks: the science of uncertainty*, Penguin Books

Sutherland V.J. & Flin R.H. (1989) *Stress at Sea: A Review of Working Conditions in the Offshore Oil and Fishing Industries*, Work and Stress 3(3): 269–85

Stone D., Patton B. & Heen S. (2000) *Difficult Conversations*, Penguin Books

Thomas M. (2005) *Lost at Sea and Lost at Home: the Predicament of Seafaring Families*, Seafarers International Research Centre, Cardiff University

Thomas M. & Bailey N. (2006) *Square pegs in round holes? Leave periods and role displacement in UK-based seafaring families*, Work, Employment & Society, Volume 20, No. 1, Sage publications

USCG (1979) *USCGC Cuyahoga, M/V Santa Cruz II (Argentine): Collision in Chesapeake Bay on 20 Oct 1978 with loss of life, US Coast Guard Marine Board of Investigation Report and Commandant's Action*, United States Coastguard Service Report No. 16732/92368, 31 Jul 1979

US DoD (1999) *MIL-STD-1472F Human Engineering Military Specifications and Standards*, US Department of Defense

Weinger M.B. & Blike G.T. (2003) *Intubation mishap*, http://webmm.ahrq.gov/case.aspx?caseID=29 (in Mar '10)

Wikipedia (2009) *MS Scandinavian Star*, http://en.wikipedia.org/wiki/MS_Scandinavian_Star (in Mar '10)

# Index